How To Own Your Own Mind

How To Own Your Own Mind

Napoleon Hill

PRABHAT PRAKASHAN

Published by
PRABHAT PRAKASHAN PVT. LTD.
4/19 Asaf Ali Road,
New Delhi-110 002 (INDIA)
e-mail: prabhatbooks@gmail.com

ISBN 978-93-5562-649-3
HOW TO OWN YOUR OWN MIND
by Napoleon Hill

Edition
2025

Price
₹ 350.00 (Rupees Three Hundred Fifty only)

Printed at
Narula Printers, Delhi

Contents

Introduction

By Don M. Green,
Executive Director, The Napoleon Hill Foundation

In 1941, Napoleon Hill created and published seventeen booklets, each one setting forth an explanation of the principles of personal achievement Mr. Hill had developed from studying great American success stories for twenty years. He was inspired to do so when, as a fledgling reporter, he interviewed the great steel magnate Andrew Carnegie, who outlined the principles of success and commissioned young Napoleon to commence an intense study of how these principles contributed to the success of the great men of the time, and of earlier times. He called the series of booklets Mental Dynamite, a phrase Mr. Carnegie had used to describe the seventeen principles.

Very shortly after the booklets were published, Pearl Harbor was attacked and America entered World War II. In preparing for and ultimately winning that war, Mental Dynamite, with so many other things of significance but less importance than the war, was set aside by the American public. It laid gathering dust in the archives of the Napoleon Hill Foundation until recently it was rediscovered, and it is now being reprinted by the foundation in book form.

This book was created by our foundation putting together three related chapters of the Mental Dynamite masterpiece. Each deals with how to think before acting, and thereby how to recognise opportunities, define one's Definite Major Purpose, and refine it until it is time to take action. When these chapters have been mastered, you will know how to own your own mind.

The first chapter sets forth the principle of Creative Vision. Andrew Carnegie explains to young Napoleon in Mr. Carnegie's study in 1908 that imagination is a primary component of it, and Mr. Carnegie provides examples of how imagination enables people to be successful in such apparently diverse activities as inventing and sales. But imagination has to be applied. 'Fleeing thoughts' and 'mere wishes' are not enough to create inventions and make sales, according to Mr. Carnegie; one must recognise opportunities, and act upon them. This is the essence of Creative Vision. Mr. Carnegie also details the ten principles of success that are used by all people who successfully apply Creative Vision.

Dr. Hill follows the extensive quotations from his interview of Mr. Carnegie with his own commentary, written some thirty-three years later. He suggests a number of ideas for improving society and industry that could benefit from the use of Creative Vision, and many are amazingly ahead of their time. He then provides a number of examples of people of the then present day who had used Creative Vision to succeed.

Considered together, the insights of Andrew Carnegie and Napoleon Hill provide a compelling lesson on how all of us can use our Creative Vision to recognise opportunities and attain our goals.

Chapter Two discusses the importance of the principle of Organised Thought. Through the use of three charts, Dr. Hill explains how one can attain and then use Organised Thought to succeed in controlling one's destiny. I believe you will realise, as I have, that these three charts deserve repeated study, and that each reading of them reveals something new. They disclose how Organised Thought, willpower, and self-discipline interact with the faculties of the mind, the five senses, the basic human motives, and other success principles to produce results when – and this is essential – action is taken. Thoughts without action are ineffective.

Dr. Hill explains how inductive and deductive reasoning and social heredity contribute to the development of Organised Thought. He explains the importance of habits, both good and bad, in influencing one's ability to achieve Organised Thought. The chapter concludes with excerpts from young Napoleon's 1908 interview with Andrew Carnegie, in which Mr. Carnegie details the positive things which can be accomplished by Organised Thought, and how its use by evil men is doomed to fail.

Chapter Three is devoted to the success principle of Controlled Attention. Controlled Attention is concentration, and more. It is the means by which one's plans are impressed on the subconscious mind. It is the process of controlling all the activities of the mind and directing them to a given end. It is essential to the implementation of Creative Vision and Organised Thought.

Dr. Hill explains how the use of other success principles, such as Going the Extra Mile, the Master Mind, and faith, can intensify the ability to develop Controlled Attention and bolster one's confidence. He provides examples of people who have combined many of the success principles with Controlled Attention to develop previously unknown solutions to problems. Dr. Hill also sets forth testimonials from many famous and successful people about how important Controlled Attention was to their lives. A common theme is that one should control attention by focussing it on one major purpose rather than many.

The chapter concludes with a further interview with Mr. Carnegie about the effects of the use of Controlled Attention. Controlled Attention leads to specialisation in one's life, which produces greater rewards than a generalised approach to a business or profession. It is essential to advancement and promotion in employment. And, when employed by the citizenry, it leads to the success of free enterprise and democracy, in contrast to a Socialist society, in which Controlled Attention, if utilised at all, ultimately withers and dies.

Napoleon Hill's best-known book is *Think and Grow Rich*. The chapters in the book before you help explain the reasoning behind that title. As Dr. Hill repeatedly emphasised, action is critical to success. But you must think before you act or your actions will be wasted.

These timeless chapters about the importance of thought before action will prove to be very instructive in helping you attain your own Definite Major Purpose. To do so, you must learn how to own your own mind, and this book will tell you how to do it.

THE power with which we think is "mental dynamite", and it can be organised and used constructively for the attainment of definite ends. If it is not organised and used through controlled habits, it may become a "mental explosive" that will literally blast one's hopes of achievement and lead to inevitable failure.

—Andrew Carnegie

CHAPTER ONE
Creative Vision

A philosopher said, 'The imagination is the workshop of man wherein is fashioned the pattern of all his achievements.' Another thinker described it as, 'The workshop of the soul wherein man's hopes and desires are made ready for material expression'.

This chapter describes the methods by which some of the great leaders of America have, through the application of Creative Vision, made the American way of life the envy of the world.

This chapter begins with the private study of Andrew Carnegie in 1908, with me, Napoleon Hill, as the student and reporter.

HILL:

Mr. Carnegie, you have said that Creative Vision is one of the principles of individual achievement. Will you analyse this principle and describe how one can make practical use of it?

CARNEGIE:

First of all, let us have a clear understanding of the meaning of the term 'Creative Vision', as we are here using it, by explaining that this is not merely another name for imagination. It is the ability to recognise opportunities and take action to benefit from them. An important element of Creative Vision is the use of the imagination.

There are two types of imaginations. One is known as synthetic imagination and the other as creative imagination.

Synthetic imagination consists of the act of combining recognised ideas, concepts, plans, facts and principles in new arrangements. The old axiom, 'There is nothing new under the sun' grew out of the fact that the majority of things which seem to be new are nothing but a rearrangement of that which is old. Practically, all the patents recorded in the Patent Office are nothing more than old ideas which have been arranged in a new order, or given a new use. Patents which do not come under this heading are known as 'basic patents' and they are the work of creative imagination; that is, they are based on newly created ideas which have not been previously used or recognised.

Creative imagination has its source, as far as science has been able to determine, in the subconscious mind, wherein exists, through some power unknown to science, the ability to perceive and interpret new ideas. It is believed, by some, that the faculty of creative imagination truly is 'the workshop of the soul'. Of one fact we can be sure, and that is the undeniable reality of the existence of a faculty of the mind through which some men perceive and interpret new ideas never before known to man. Later, I shall cite well-known examples of such ability. Moreover, I shall endeavour to describe how this ability may be developed and made to serve practical ends.

HILL:

Which of the two types of imaginations is used more often in the field of industry, and in the ordinary walks of life?

CARNEGIE:

Synthetic imagination is more commonly used. Creative imagination, as the name implies, is used only by those who have attained the means to apply this unusual skill.

HILL:

Will you mention examples of the application of both types of imagination, giving as many of the details as possible in order that the practical methods of application of these principles may be understood?

CARNEGIE:

Well, let us take the work of Thomas A. Edison, for example. By studying his achievements we shall see how he made use of both types of imaginations, although he used the synthetic type more often.

His first invention to attract worldwide attention was created by bringing together, in a new combination, two old and well-known principles. I refer to the incandescent electric lamp, the perfection of which was attained only after Mr. Edison had tried more than ten thousand different combinations of old ideas without satisfactory results.

HILL:

Do you mean, Mr. Carnegie, that Mr. Edison had the persistence to keep on trying in the face of ten thousand failures?

CARNEGIE:

Yes, I mean just that! And I may as well here call your attention to the fact that men with a keen sense of imagination seldom quit trying until they find the answer to their problems.

Mr. Edison perfected the incandescent electric lamp by combining two well-known principles in a new way. The first of these principles was the established fact that by applying electric energy to both ends of a piece of wire, a resistance is established through which the wire becomes heated to a white glow that will produce light. That principle had been known long before the time of Mr. Edison's experiments with the electric lamp, but the trouble arose from the fact that no way had been found to control the heat. Perhaps the facts would be better understood if I said that no form of metal or other substance had been found that could carry the necessary amount of heat to make a satisfactory light for more than a few seconds. The intense heat of electricity soon burned out the metal.

After trying every known substance he could find, without discovering anything that would serve the desired purpose, Mr. Edison stumbled upon another well-known principle which proved to be the answer to his problem. I say he 'stumbled' upon it, but perhaps that is not the precise way the principle came to his attention. Of that I shall have more to say later on. At any rate, there came into his mind the well-known principle by which charcoal is produced, and he recognised in it the answer to the problem that had caused him more than ten thousand failures.

Briefly explained, charcoal is produced by placing a pile of wood on the ground, setting it on fire, and then covering the whole pile with dirt. The dirt permits just enough air to pass through to the fire to keep it alive and smoldering but not enough to enable the fire to blaze. The smoldering process continues until the wood becomes charred through and through, leaving the log intact, in the form of a substance known as charcoal.

You, of course, learned, in the study of physics, that where there is no oxygen, there can be no fire; that by controlling the inflow of oxygen, the amount of heat of the fire can be controlled proportionately.

Mr. Edison had known of this principle long before he began experimenting with the electric lamp, but not until he had gone through thousands of tests did he think of it as being the principle for which he was searching.

As soon as this principle was recognised as the one for which he was searching, he went into his laboratory, placed a coiled wire in a bottle, pumped out all the air, sealed the bottle with wax, applied the electric energy to the two ends of the wire, and lo! the world's first successful incandescent electric lamp was born. The crudely constructed lamp burned for more than eight hours. Of course, it is obvious as to what had happened. By placing the wire in a vacuum that contained no oxygen, it could be heated sufficiently to cause it to produce a light without its burning out entirely, as it had done when left in the open air. That same principle is used in the making of all incandescent electric lamps today, although the method has been greatly refined until the modern electric lamp is much more efficient than it was when Edison first discovered how to control the heat.

Now, let us go back to the question as to how Mr. Edison came to think of combining these two old principles in a new way. I said he 'stumbled' upon the idea of using the charcoal principle as a means of controlling the heat of the electric energy. But that is not exactly the way this idea occurred to him.

Here begins, then, the entry into the picture of the principle of creative imagination. By his repetition of thought in connection with his problem, carried on over a long period of time, through thousands of experiments, Mr. Edison either consciously or unconsciously charged his subconscious mind with a clear picture of his problem, and, by some queer power which no one understands, his subconscious mind handed over to him the solution to his problem, in the form of a 'hunch' that caused him to think of the charcoal principle.

In describing the experience many years afterwards, Mr. Edison said that when the 'hunch' came to him he recognised it immediately as being the missing link for which he had been searching. Moreover, he felt assured it would work, even before he tested it. He made the further significant statement that when the idea of using the charcoal principle 'flashed into his mind', it brought with it a feeling of assurance of its suitability such as did not accompany any one of the other thousands of similar ideas he had tested, through synthetic imagination.

From this statement, we may draw the conclusion that the subconscious mind not only has the power to create the solution to problems, but it also has a means of forcing one to recognise the solution when it is presented to the conscious mind.

> Wherever you find a prosperous business, you will come across some individual who has **Creative Vision.**

HILL:

From what you have said, Mr. Carnegie, I conclude that persistence was of the essence of Mr. Edison's discovery of the solution to his problem.

CARNEGIE:

Yes, and some other factors, too. First of all, he began his research with definiteness of purpose, thus applying perhaps the most important of the principles of individual achievement. He knew the nature of his problem, but equally as important as this, he was determined to find its solution.

Therefore, he backed his definiteness of purpose with an obsessional desire for its attainment. Obsessional desire is the state of mind which serves to clear the mind of fear and doubt and self-imposed limitations, thereby opening the way for that state of mind known as Faith. By his refusal to accept defeat, through more than ten thousand failures, Mr. Edison prepared his mind for the application of Faith.

HILL:

Were all of Mr. Edison's inventions created through the joint application of creative imagination and synthetic imagination, as in the case of the incandescent electric lamp?

CARNEGIE:

Oh, no! Not by any means. The majority of his inventions were created solely through the aid of synthetic imagination, by the trial and error method of experimentation. But he did complete one invention solely through the aid of creative imagination, and as far as I know, this was the only invention he perfected through this principle alone. I have reference to the phonograph. That was a new idea. No one before Edison, as far as is known, had ever produced a machine that would record and reproduce the vibrations of sound.

HILL:

What technique did Mr. Edison use in the application of creative imagination in perfecting the talking machine?

CARNEGIE:

The technique was very simple. He impressed his subconscious mind with the idea of a talking machine and there passed over to his conscious mind a perfect plan for the building of such a machine.

HILL:

Do you mean that Edison relied on creative imagination entirely?

CARNEGIE:

Yes, entirely! And one of the strange features of this particular invention of Mr. Edison is the fact that the plan which his subconscious mind yielded to him worked almost from the first attempt to apply it. The idea of how such a machine could be produced 'flashed' into Edison's mind. He sat down then and there and drew a rough picture of the machine, handed it to his model maker and asked him to produce the machine, and, in a matter of hours, it had been finished, tested, and lo! it worked. Of course, the machine was crude, but it was sufficient to prove that Edison's creative imagination had not failed him.

HILL:

You say that Mr. Edison "impressed his subconscious

mind" with the idea of a talking machine. Now, how did he go about doing this, and how long did it require before his subconscious mind handed over to him the working principle of the machine?

CARNEGIE:

I am not sure that Mr. Edison stated exactly how long he had been thinking of such a machine before his subconscious mind picked up his thoughts and translated them into a perfected plan, but I am under the impression it was not more than a few weeks, at most. Perhaps not more than a few days. His method of impressing his subconscious mind with his desire consisted of the simple procedure of converting that desire into an obsession. That is, the thought of a machine that would record and reproduce sound became the dominating thought of his mind. He focussed his mind on it, through concentration of his interest, and made it the major occupant of his mind from day to day until this form of auto-suggestion penetrated his subconscious mind and registered a clear picture of his desire.

HILL:

Is that the way one connects the conscious mind with the subconscious, Mr. Carnegie?

CARNEGIE:

Yes, that is the simplest known method. You see, therefore, why I have emphasised the importance of intensifying one's desires until they become obsessional. A deep, burning desire is picked up by the subconscious and acted upon much more definitely and quickly than an ordinary desire. A mere wish appears to make no impression on the subconscious!

Many people become confused as to the difference between a wish and a burning desire which has been stimulated into obsessional proportions by the repetition of thought in connection with the desire.

HILL:

If I understand you correctly, Mr. Carnegie, the element of repetition is important. Why?

CARNEGIE:

Because repetition of thought creates 'thought habits' in the mind which cause the mind to go right on working on an idea without one's conscious effort. Apparently, the subconscious concerns itself first with those thoughts which have become habits and especially if the thoughts have been strongly emotionalised by a deep and burning desire for their realisation.

HILL:

Then can anyone make use of creative imagination by the simple process of charging his subconscious mind with definite desires?

CARNEGIE:

Yes, there is nothing to hinder anyone from using this principle, but you must remember that practical results are obtained only by those who have gained discipline over their thought habits, through the process of concentration of interest and desire. Fleeting thoughts which come and go intermittently, and mere wishes, which are about the extent of the average person's thinking, make no impression whatsoever on the subconscious mind.

HILL:

Will you mention some additional examples of the practical application of the two types of imagination?

CARNEGIE:

Well, take the experience of Henry Ford, in connection with his perfection of a self-propelled vehicle, for example. The idea of such a vehicle was first suggested to him by a steam-propelled tractor that was being used to haul a threshing machine. From the first time that he saw the tractor, his mind began to work on the idea of a horseless buggy.

At first, he used only the principle of synthetic imagination by centring his mind on ways and means of converting the steam tractor into a rapid-moving vehicle for the transportation of passengers. The idea became obsessional with him, and it had the effect of conveying his burning desire to his subconscious mind where it was picked up and acted upon. The action of the subconscious mind suggested to him the use of an internal combustion engine to take the place of the steam engine, and he went to work immediately on the creation of such an engine. Of course, he had the experiments of other men in connection with internal combustion gas engines as a guide, but his problem was to find a way to convey the power of the engine to the wheels of a vehicle. He kept his mind charged with his major purpose until, step by step, his subconscious mind presented him with ideas with which he perfected the planetary system of power transmission which enabled him to perfect his first working model of an automobile.

HILL:

Will you describe the major factors which entered into the modus operandi of Mr. Ford's mind while he was perfecting the automobile?

CARNEGIE:

Yes, that will be very easy. And when I describe them, you will have a clear understanding of the working principles used by all successful men, as well as a clear picture of the Ford mind, viz.:

(a) Mr. Ford was motivated by a definite purpose, which is the first step in all individual achievements.

(b) He stimulated his purpose into an obsession by concentrating his thoughts upon it.

(c) He converted his purpose into definite plans, through the principle of Organised Individual Endeavour, and put his plans into action with unabating persistence.

(d) He made use of the Master Mind principle, first, by the harmonious aid of his wife, and second, by gaining counsel from others who had experimented with internal combustion engines and methods of power transmission. Still later, of course, when he began to produce automobiles for sale, he made a still more extensive use of the Master Mind principle by allying himself with the Dodge brothers and other mechanics and engineers skilled in the sort of mechanical problems he had to solve.

(e) Back of all this effort was the power of Applied Faith, which he acquired as the result of his intense desire for achievement in connection with his Definite Major Purpose.

HILL:

Summarised briefly, Mr. Ford's success was due to his having adopted a Definite Major Purpose which he fanned into a white heat flame of obsession, thus leading to the stimulation of both the faculties of synthetic imagination and creative imagination. Does that state the facts?

CARNEGIE:

That tells the story in one sentence! The part of the story that should be emphasised is the fact that Mr. Ford moved with persistence! At first, he met with one form of defeat after another. One of his major difficulties was lack of capital with which to carry on his research, before he perfected his automobile. After that came a still greater difficulty in connection with procuring the necessary operating capital to produce his automobiles in quantity production. Then followed a series of difficulties, such as disagreements with the members of his Master Mind group, and other similar problems, all of which called for persistence and determination. These qualities Mr. Ford possesses, and I think we might say that he owes his success to his ability to know exactly what he wants and his capacity to stand by his wants with unrelenting persistence.

If one single quality stands out in the Ford character, above all others, it is his capacity for persistence. Let me remind you, again, that definiteness of purpose, backed with a form of persistence, that assumes the proportion of an obsession, is the greatest of all stimulants of both the synthetic and the creative forms of imagination. The mind of man is provided with a power which forces the subconscious mind to accept and to act upon obsessional desires that are definitely planned.

HILL:

Will you now cite some other examples of the practical application of imagination?

CARNEGIE:

Take, for example, Dr. Alexander Graham Bell's research in connection with the modern telephone. Here we have an example of the use of creative imagination, for Bell's invention was new. Let us say that he, like Edison, 'stumbled' upon the principle that made the telephone practical, while searching for some mechanical device with which he could create a hearing aid for his wife, whose hearing was impaired.

Here, again, we find a man who was inspired by a definite purpose which assumed obsessional proportions. His keen sympathy for his wife was the factor that gave obsessional force to his purpose. In this case, as in all others where men give obsessional proportions to their desires, a definite motive was behind his desire. Motive is the beginning of all desires.

Through a long period of research that is too involved in details for description here, Dr. Bell's subconscious mind finally presented him with an idea which served his purpose. It became known to the scientific world as Bell's experiment, the substance of which was this:

A ray of light is cast upon a plate of selenium, which sends the ray back to another plate – some distance away – of the same metal. This latter communicates with a galvanic battery, to which a telephone is attached. The words uttered behind the first plate are distinctly heard through the telephone at the end of the second plate. The ray of light, accordingly, has served as a telephone wire. The sound waves have become transformed into light waves, the latter into galvanic waves, and these have become once again sound waves.

Thus, a new principle for conveying sound waves was uncovered. It has been claimed that the principle, in part, was suggested to Dr. Bell by the experiments of a man by the name of Dolbear. There was a lawsuit over the priority of right to the principle, but Mr. Dolbear lost the suit, and Dr. Bell was declared to have been the discoverer of the working principle of the modern telephone.

At any rate, Dr. Bell's desire for a mechanical hearing aid for his wife, backed by a persistent search for such a device, led to the discovery of the principle he needed. It must be remembered that the subconscious mind makes use of every practical means available for revealing knowledge to those seeking it with obsessional desire. It performs no miracles, but it makes intelligent use of all practical media available in carrying out its purpose.

HILL:

Now, Mr. Carnegie, let us get away from the field of invention and see how the principle of imagination may be applied in the less complicated fields of endeavour.

CARNEGIE:

Very well, take, for example, the first great mail-order house that was established in the United States. Here we have a fine example of synthetic imagination applied to merchandising.

A telegraph operator with whom I formerly worked found that he had extra time on his hands which he could not use in connection with his duties as railroad telegrapher. Being a man with an inquisitive type of mind, he began to search for something he could do that would keep him occupied and, at the same time, add to his income. Here, again, the question of motive entered the picture, the motive of financial gain.

After having turned the matter over in his mind for several months, he envisioned a profitable outlet for his efforts by using the idle telegraph line for the purpose of selling watches to his fellow operators in his division. So, he ordered half-a-dozen watches, at wholesale rates, and began to offer them for sale. The idea caught fire from the very beginning. In a very short time, he had sold all six of the watches. Then, spurred on by his success, his imagination began to expand until he took on other items of jewellery. Everything went well, and he was doing a land-office business, until his superintendent found out what he was up to and fired him on the spot.

Every adversity brings with it the seed of an equivalent benefit! Out of this telegrapher's adversity was born the first great mail-order house. He switched his method of selling from telegraphy to the mails, using at first a mimeographed catalogue of his wares. Moreover, he added others outside the field of telegraphers to his list of prospective buyers, mainly people living in the villages and rural districts. In a little while, his business had grown to where he could afford a printed catalogue illustrated with pictures of his merchandise. From that point on, the story is known to millions of people throughout the United States, who now purchase merchandise from the mail-order house he established.

He then took a partner into the business with him, thereby making use of the Master Mind principle. This partner proved to be a veritable gold mine because he had a keen sense of advertising. Several years later, the business was sold out to a corporation at a price which made its owners multimillionaires. That was the beginning of mail-order merchandising on a large scale.

Now, there was nothing very mysterious about this man's success. He simply put his mind to work on a definite purpose and kept behind that purpose until it made him rich. He did not create anything new. He merely put an old idea to a new use. In this manner, many of the great fortunes have been accumulated.

HILL:

If I understand you correctly, Mr. Carnegie, the telegraph operator applied only the principle of synthetic imagination. Is that correct?

CARNEGIE:

Yes, that is it. You see, he did nothing except apply the principle of merchandising in a new way but do not forget that this is about all that most successful men do. Rarely do men create new ideas, through the application of creative imagination, as Dr. Bell and Mr. Edison did.

Now let us take the modern railroad refrigerator car, for example. The man who first made practical application of this principle revolutionised the meat-packing business. He was a packer whose business was limited due to the fact that he could ship fresh meat only a short distance. Motivated by a desire to extend his business over a greater territory, he began to search for a suitable method.

A man generally finds whatever he is looking for if he gives his desire obsessional proportions. Well, this packer was motivated by the desire for larger financial gains. So, he kept his mind on his problem until it occurred to him to convert an ordinary railroad boxcar into an oversized icebox. There was nothing left to be done except to go to work and experiment with the idea, which he proceeded to do. The plan worked satisfactorily, although the first refrigerator car was a very crude affair. He kept on improving his idea until he had refined it into the modern refrigerator car, as we know it today. His idea not only helped him to extend his meat business almost without limitation, but it gave a new impetus to the sale and distribution of other lines of merchandise, particularly fruits and vegetables, until today that single idea has added hundreds of millions of dollars of wealth to individuals, corporations, and the nation as a whole.

The refrigerator car was brought into existence solely by the application of synthetic imagination, through the simple process of placing an icebox on wheels, so to speak.

George Pullman performed a similar feat by placing beds in railroad coaches, thus converting them into sleeping quarters. There was nothing new about either the beds or the rail-road coaches; but the idea of combining these two types of service was new. The new combination made the man who created it an immense fortune, to say nothing of providing thousands of jobs for others and a desirable service for the travelling public, for which it continues to pay a huge sum annually. Ideas such as these are the products of imagination. The man who trains his mind to create ideas, or to give old ideas a new and better use is well on the road towards economic independence.

Back of these ideas was the personal initiative of the men who created them, plus the principle of Organised Individual Endeavour through which they were made practical. Both the sleeping car and the refrigerator car had to be promoted and sold, thus necessitating the investment of large amounts of capital. Both of these ideas, and all other similar ideas that are made practical, require the application of some combination of the principles of individual achievement; but in final analysis, such ideas generally can be traced back to their originating source, in the imagination of one person.

HILL:

Will you name the success principles which are most commonly used by those who apply the principle of imagination?

CARNEGIE:

Well, that depends somewhat on the nature of the application that is to be made of imagination, and the person making it, but generally speaking, the following are the principles which are more often allied with imagination:

(a) Definiteness of purpose. The motive which more commonly serves to stimulate the imagination is that of a desire for financial gain. The profit motive has been, without a doubt, the greatest inspiration to the men who have developed industrial America.

(b) The Master Mind principle, through which men go into a huddle and frankly exchange thoughts with the object of solving business or professional problems, is also a great stimulation of the imagination. It was this principle, more than all others, through which the steel industry of which I was the founder became prosperous. The so-called 'round table' is a great institution. When men sit down and begin to pool their ideas, in a spirit of harmony and oneness of purpose, they soon find a solution to most of the problems that confront them, no matter what business they may be engaged in, or what may be the nature of their problems.

(c) Going the Extra Mile comes in prominently for its share of credit as a stimulant to the imagination. When a man makes it a habit to do more than he is paid for, he generally begins to draw upon his imagination for new sources through which to render this sort of service. This fact alone would be sufficient compensation for Going the Extra Mile, even if there were not still greater benefits available.

(d) Applied Faith is a definite source of stimulation of the imagination. Moreover, it is essential in connection with the stimulation and application of creative imagination. Men with little or no faith will never receive the benefits of creative imagination.

(e) Organised Individual Endeavour depends directly upon the application of imagination for its effectiveness, as all forms of definite planning are carried on through imagination.

> WHEN you pray, do not ask for more blessings; but ask for more wisdom that you may better understand and enjoy the blessings you already have.

There are many other sources of stimulation of the imagination, but these five are on the 'must' list.

Fear sometimes stimulates the imagination, while, of course, at other times, it paralyses the imagination. When a man is in great danger, his imagination often performs seemingly superhuman feats; especially where self-preservation is the motive.

Failure and temporary defeat sometimes have the effect of stirring one's imagination, although more often they have the opposite effect.

The question method which master salesmen often resort to has the effect of arousing the imagination and putting it to work, and the reason for this is obvious. By asking questions, the salesman forces his prospective buyer to think. Moreover, he chooses the line of thought to be engaged in, by the adroitness of his questions.

Curiosity often stimulates imagination to a high pitch. Curiosity, growing out of death and the uncertainty of life, and the unknown and perhaps unknowable facts of immortality, has been the chief source of inspiration, out of which all the religions have grown.

Self-expression, through speaking and writing, is a never-ending source of stimulation of the imagination, as are many other forms of action. The very moment a man begins to organise his thoughts for the purpose of expression, whether through words or deeds, he starts his imagination to work. For this reason, children should be encouraged to give free expression to their thoughts, as this develops imagination early in life.

Hunger is a universal source of inspiration of imagination. When a man needs food, his imagination goes to work automatically, without any form of urge. In the lower order of life, instinct goes to work in the face of hunger, and I have known of ingenious applications of instinct under such an urge.

Thus, we see that wherever we touch life, whether in man or the lower orders of organised life, imagination and instinct may be found as essential parts of the individual's working equipment.

Concentration of attention on a definite problem or object tends to put the imagination to work immediately. Witness, for example, the astounding achievements of Dr. Elmer R. Gates, who created hundreds of useful inventions by 'sitting for ideas'. The same principle was used by Thomas A. Edison and Dr. Alexander Graham Bell. By fixing their minds on definite objectives, through definiteness of purpose, they put creative imagination to work with far-reaching results.

Scientists, and sometimes laymen, put their imaginations to work by setting up hypotheses of facts or ideas which, for the time being, they assume to exist. Scientific research and experiment would hardly be practical if hypothetical cases were not utilised, as often the facts for which they are searching are entirely unknown. Lawyers and trial judges often resort to the use of hypotheses in order to establish facts that cannot be uncovered through any other source. The chemist and the physicist resort to the same method when searching for unknown facts. And so does the doctor, when other means of diagnosis of disease fail him. Detectives often work entirely through the aid of hypotheses in the solution of crime.

Right after the War Between the States, a foundry owner purchased a large quantity of unused cannonballs which he wished to melt for other uses. Before the balls could be melted conveniently, they had to be broken into small pieces. There seemed no way to do the job except by hiring men to break the balls with heavy hammers, until a man with imagination came along, looked the cannonballs over, discovered that they were hollow inside, and made a very low bid for breaking the entire lot. Moreover, he astonished the foundryman by guaranteeing to break the entire lot himself, and to do it by the following morning.

He was given the contract, after which he turned all the balls. So, the small opening in each appeared on the top side. Then, to the amazement of everyone, he calmly filled the balls with water. The night was very cold, and the following morning, the foundryman found every ball nicely broken by the expansion of the frozen contents. His only comment was, "Why didn't I think of that in the first place?"

We all have occasion, at times, to wonder why we hadn't used our own imagination when we see others making profitable use of theirs.

HILL:

Why is it that so few people appear to have a well-developed imagination? Is the capacity for a keen imagination a matter of heredity, Mr. Carnegie?

CARNEGIE:

No, the faculty of imagination, like all other faculties of the mind, can be developed through use. The reason so many people seem not to have a keen imagination is obvious. Most people allow the faculty of imagination to atrophy, through neglect.

HILL:

Inasmuch as everyone must use salesmanship, in one way or another, will you illustrate how imagination can be used in selling?

CARNEGIE:

Yes, I can give you an endless number of examples of this sort. Take the case of a life insurance agent whom I know, for instance. He began selling insurance after an accident which incapacitated him for any sort of heavy manual labour, and within a year, he became the high man in sales in the entire United States in his company.

I will give you one illustration that will tell the story of his success. But, before I do so, I think I should tell you that this man became a master at applying the Master Mind principle. He also became equally proficient in applying many of the other principles of achievement, among them Organised Thought.

One day he walked into the office of a very distinguished and wealthy lawyer and came out, within half-an-hour, with an application for a million-dollar policy on the lawyer's life, although the lawyer was known to have refused to purchase insurance from a half dozen or more of the ablest insurance men of the city in which he lived.

And this is the way he did it:

He carried with him a fully illustrated newspaper feature story of the lawyer's activities, set in type with a heavy streamer headline which read: "Prominent Lawyer Insures His Brains for a Million Dollars!"

The story told how the lawyer had come up from the bottom, through his unusual skill as a corporation attorney, until he was in a position where he commanded the most select clientele in New York City. The story was well written. It carried pictures of the lawyer and the members of his family, including a picture of his Long Island estate.

He handed the story to the lawyer and said, "I have made arrangements for this story to be released in over a hundred newspapers the moment you prove that you can pass the necessary physical examination. I hardly need to suggest to a man of your intelligence that the story will bring you enough new clients to more than pay the premium on the insurance policy."

The lawyer sat down and read the story carefully. When he had finished, he asked how the insurance man had procured so much information about him, and how he managed to get those pictures of his family.

"Oh," replied the insurance man, "that was easy. I simply made arrangements with a newspaper syndicate to do the job."

The lawyer read the story a second time, made a few corrections in it, handed it back, and said, "Let's have your application blank." The sale was closed in a few minutes, but more than three months of preparation went into it before the insurance agent made his call. He left no detail unattended. He made it his business to find out all about the lawyer before the story was written, and saw to it that the story was so prepared that it got under the lawyer's skin at his weakest point, which was his desire for publicity.

What he really sold the lawyer was not an insurance policy on his life, but an insurance policy on his vanity! That streamer headline turned the trick. Moreover, the salesman not only earned a fat premium on the sale, but he also received $500 from the newspaper syndicate for the exclusive use of the story.

Now, that was imagination, or I miss my guess!

Salesmen with imagination often sell something entirely different from that which they appear to be selling. The experience of Dr. Harper, a former president of the University of Chicago, aptly illustrates what I mean.

Dr. Harper was one of the greatest "endowment getters" the educational world has ever known. He took a notion to build a new building on the campus that required a million-dollar endowment. If you wish to see imagination as it is employed by a master, observe the technique through which he got his million dollars. Observe, also, how many of the principles of individual achievement he applied in addition to imagination.

First of all, he chose his prospective donors with adroitness, confining the number to two well-known Chicago men, both of whom were quite able to donate a million dollars.

It could not have been purely accidental that these two men were known to be bitter enemies. One was a professional politician and the other was the head of the Chicago street railway system. For years, these two men had been fighting each other, a fact which would have meant nothing to anyone with less imagination than Dr. Harper possessed.

One day, precisely at twelve o'clock, Dr. Harper strolled into the office of the streetcar magnate, found no one on duty at the outer door (which was exactly as he expected the situation to be), and walked into the streetcar man's private office unannounced.

The magnate looked up from his desk, but before he had time to protest, the super-salesman said, "I beg your pardon for walking in unannounced, but I found no one in the outer office. My name is Dr. Harper, and I just called to see you for a minute."

"Please be seated," said the streetcar man.

"No, thank you," replied the educator, "I have only a minute, so I will tell you what I have in mind and then be on my way. I have been thinking, for some time, that the University of Chicago should do something to recognise you for the wonderful job you have done in giving the city the finest street railway system in America, and I had in mind honouring you with a building on the campus to be named for you. When I mentioned the matter to our board, one of the members had the same idea; but he wanted us to honour (naming the streetcar man's enemy). So, I just came in to tell you what had happened, with the hope that you might find some way to help me defeat this board member's plan."

"Well!" exclaimed the streetcar man. "That is an interesting idea. Do please be seated and let us see what we can work out, will you?"

"I am very sorry," the educator apologised, "but I have another engagement in a few minutes and I must hurry on to it; but I tell you what I suggest. You think the matter over during the night and telephone me in the morning if any plan comes to mind that might help me to get the right man's name on that building. Good day, sir!"

Without leaving any opening for further conversation, the master of imagination bowed himself out.

Th next morning when he arrived at his office at the university, he found the streetcar man awaiting him. The two men walked inside, remained there about an hour, after which they walked out again, both of them smiling. Dr. Harper carried a check in his hands, waving it back and forth in the air to blot it. The check was for one million dollars.

The streetcar man had found a way to beat his enemy to the draw, as the clever Dr. Harper figured he would do. Moreover, he had sealed the bargain by delivering the money with the understanding that Dr. Harper would become personally responsible for its acceptance.

Now, if it is salesmanship based on imagination that you want, here you have it. Those who knew the streetcar man best said that no other plan that could have been conceived would have succeeded. And that is another thing about these men who develop imagination through its use; they generally know the precise plan that will work. This is an essential part of their training.

HILL:

Was Dr. Harper's success solely the result of his understanding and use of imagination, or did other factors enter into it?

CARNEGIE:

In his case, I would say that he used Creative Vision, and not just imagination alone.

HILL:

What is the difference between imagination and Creative Vision? The two terms appear to be synonymous.

CARNEGIE:

No, they are not the same. Creative Vision is an acquired ability through which one does two very important things, viz.: First, he becomes keenly alert in recognising opportunities favorable to the attainment of his aims and purposes; second, he develops the habit of embracing these opportunities and acting upon them through Organised Individual Endeavour.

> EDISON had the persistence to keep on trying in the face of ten thousand failures. —Andrew Carnegie

A man may have a very keen imagination in connection with some specialised line of work, or some technical subject; such, for example, as the inventor; but he may be entirely lacking in the Creative Vision and action necessary to commercialise his inventive ability. We find this to be true of many inventors.

A man may have keen imagination as an artist, as, in fact, most artists do have, yet be entirely lacking in the Creative Vision necessary to make a business success of his artistic ability. Do you see the point?

HILL:

Yes, I see the point plainly. What other factors are associated with Creative Vision?

CARNEGIE:

Well, the best answer I can give you is to describe the procedure of the man who has Creative Vision. You will observe, from my description, that Creative Vision overlaps many of the other principles of individual achievement.

First, the man with Creative Vision (such a man as Dr. Harper) develops the alertness of mind to recognise opportunities favourable to his own advancement.

Second, he moves with definiteness of purpose in embracing opportunities.

Third, he plans every move he makes, through Organised Endeavour.

Fourth, he recognises and uses the Master Mind principle, through which he provides himself with the ability and the knowledge of others.

Fifth, he removes limitations from his own mind by recognising and using Applied Faith, thereby opening his mind for the guidance of Infinite Intelligence. No man may possess Creative Vision without the aid of Faith, and this for the reason that Faith is of the essence of creative ability.

Sixth, he adopts and follows the habit of Going the Extra Mile, thereby attracting favourable opportunities to himself.

Seventh, he keeps his mind definitely attuned to the circumstances and conditions of those around him, observing not only the general trend of the times, but watching closely the problems, needs and desires of people in general.

Eighth, he moves on his own personal initiative, without being urged to do so.

Ninth, he assumes full responsibility for his own deeds and depends upon the soundness of his own judgement, in the formation of his plans, having first wisely availed himself of the counsel of others, through the Master Mind principle.

Tenth, he develops and uses both the faculties of synthetic imagination and creative imagination. Take notice, however, that these two factors constitute but one-tenth of the principles used by the man of Creative Vision.

I think this should give you a fair understanding of the difference between imagination and Creative Vision.

HILL:

Yes, the difference is clear. It is also very great! I suppose this answers my question as to why there are so few people who appear to use imagination.

CARNEGIE:

What you really meant to say was that there are so few people who use Creative Vision! All normal people use imagination, to one extent or another; but few make use of Creative Vision. As I have clearly shown, imagination is but one of the factors of Creative Vision.

Industrial America, as we know it today, is the handiwork of men with Creative Vision. When men with this sort of vision put money to work, they create wealth in its most useful form: wealth in the form of employment, wealth in the form of high standards of living, wealth in the form of education embracing experience and skill in every walk of life.

Men with Creative Vision are builders. They never tear down. They are positive, not negative. They build our great railway systems; they construct our skyscrapers and extend the boundaries of our great metropolitan cities; they gave us the telephone, and the airplane, and the automobile, and the multifarious devices for harnessing and using electricity. They also gave us the most efficient system of government known to the civilised world, under which every American citizen has the privilege of exercising his personal initiative to the fullest extent of his Creative Vision and his individual ability.

When you look under the surface of this thing called Creative Vision, you find it to be the forerunner of civilisation. Back through the ages, we may find evidence that civilisation has evolved through the leadership of a relatively small number of men. These were men with Creative Vision whose alertness of mind kept them always ahead of the masses. Such men were Samuel Adams, Richard Henry Lee, Thomas Jefferson, John Hancock, George Washington, Thomas Paine, and the other great patriots of their time who risked life and fortune to give birth to the America we know today.

Measure these men by their deeds and see how definitely they used the ten factors of Creative Vision which I have mentioned.

HILL:

What causes men to develop Creative Vision, Mr. Carnegie? Or, is this an inborn trait with which only a few men are gifted?

CARNEGIE:

I can answer your question best by referring you to the basic motives behind all actions. Motive is the mainspring of all human endeavour. Take any man who is known to possess Creative Vision, analyse him carefully, and you find that he has been spurred on by some impelling motive.

The major motive of the men who gave this nation its liberty was the desire for liberty and freedom.

The motive of the great industrial leaders who gave us our industrial America was a desire for financial gain, popularly known as the "profit motive". In many instances, these men were moved by the desire for self-expression, which is another of the basic motives. But always there was present a definite motive which inspired our leaders to action.

One of the greatest factors of the American way of life is that our entire economic system and our form of government are so designed and operated that they provide premiums and rewards for the expression of personal initiative. The 'profit motive' and personal initiative are inseparable. Under the American way of life, the 'profit motive' is the greatest of all the motives which inspire personal initiative. If this motive were killed off, or subdued, the greatest source of our national wealth would be likewise depreciated.

I wish to emphasise this point because I can see a tendency towards habits and practices which discourage men from exercising their personal initiative. Some men have the false notion that by limiting the amount of work one man is permitted to do, new jobs are created. Without going into a detailed analysis of this philosophy, I can tell you that the man who permits anyone to limit the amount of service he renders thereby fixes a definite limitation upon the amount he may earn, and that limitation usually is somewhere in the neighbourhood of the bare necessities of life, and no more.

Men with Creative Vision never limit the amount of service they render. On the contrary, they extend their services in every direction possible, by Going the Extra Mile. There is no other way by which a man can make the fullest use of his privilege of personal initiative.

To get more from life, one must give more!

This is a truism from which no man can escape. Nature fixed it in all natural laws; therefore, it is not a man-made rule.

HILL:

Then it would be unfortunate if our form of government were so changed that it would discourage people of the United States from embracing and acting upon this law.

CARNEGIE:

Not merely unfortunate, but tragic! If you examine the Foundation Stones of Americanism carefully, you will see that the entire American way of life provides every individual with adequate rewards for embracing and using the best motives.

Nowhere in the economic set-up will you find anything that discourages men from backing their personal initiative with these motives. And I may add that our present high standard of living is due entirely to the fact that the American form of government has been so designed that it encourages individuals to use these motives.

HILL:

Do you believe, Mr. Carnegie, that the American way of life, as it has been provided under our form of government, is responsible for the fact that this nation is distinguished throughout the world because of the great number of men with Creative Vision of whom we can boast?

CARNEGIE:

You have hit the nail right on the head by that question. Yes, without a doubt, the supremacy of American industry and our leadership in other directions are due to the encouragement provided by our form of government. Read the Constitution of the United States carefully and observe, with significance, how clearly it has provided for the protection of the right of free enterprise and the privilege of personal initiative.

Now examine, carefully, the elements of Creative Vision and note how all of these lead, inevitably, to the question of personal initiative. Take that privilege away from a man, or limit it in any manner, and you strike at the very heart of the greatest privilege that is available to the American people. It has been the personal initiative of the great leaders that has made America the envy of the rest of the world. From this conclusion, there is no escape, try as we may to avoid it.

HILL:

I understand that you encouraged the members of your Master Mind group to become wealthy. Your policy of overpaying your associates for Going the Extra Mile was your method of encouraging personal initiative. Is that the idea?

CARNEGIE:

That's the idea precisely! There is only one satisfactory way to get men to do their best, and that is by setting up before them a motive which is sufficiently attractive to inspire them to act on their own initiative. The nature and scope of the motive must be measured by the potential ability and the personal characteristics of the man whom it is intended to inspire. This is usually determined by an individual's ambitions and personal limitations. Some men aspire only to acquire economic security. Still others are self-limited by a desire for only the necessities of life. Others want great riches, and they can be moved by no other motive than that of abundance.

However, I must tell you that of all the thousands of associate workers who have been connected with my industry, less than fifty of them were motivated by the desire for great riches. I helped more than forty of these to attain the object of their desires by becoming millionaires or better. Eight or ten others had the desire for great riches, but they fell short of attaining their desire because they neglected to apply the rules of individual achievement which would have entitled them to attain it.

I think it may be interesting to know that most of those who fell by the wayside, after they had gone a long distance towards the attainment of their desire, did so because they became neglectful of the principle of Going the Extra Mile. Success had the reverse effect on them to that which it should have had. It caused them to begin thinking they should be paid for what they knew instead of that which they did, or induced others to do. This is a mistake which is fatal to many who make a good start towards success, but slow down when they come within sight of it.

HILL:

Mr. Carnegie, aren't there some employers who set

arbitrary limitations on the amount of money they will permit their associate workers to make?

CARNEGIE:

Yes, there are many such, but name me one of them, if you can, who has ever become an outstanding success in his field. Success is something which a man has to give away in order to keep it. The man who helps the greatest number of others to succeed is, himself, the greatest success. It has been so since the dawn of civilisation. It will always be so. The founders of this nation recognised this truth and wrote it into the Constitution of the United States, by providing every citizen with the utmost of personal privileges that could be conceived, with the object of inspiring individuals to aim high and acquire much.

HILL:

Would you say that the men who wrote the Constitution of the United States were the men of Creative Vision?

CARNEGIE:

Yes, and they were the most outstanding men in this respect that this nation or any other has ever known. Without Creative Vision, they could not have had the foresight and the wisdom to prepare a constitution that gives equal rights to all men. Those men were statesmen in the true sense of the word. Today we have many politicians, but few statesmen.

HILL:

What has happened, Mr. Carnegie, that has brought about the shortage of great statesmen, such as those who gave birth to this nation?

CARNEGIE:

I'll tell you what has happened. This country has become so rich and prosperous, and personal liberty and freedom have become so cheap, that men are no longer motivated by the desire for personal freedom, as were the statesmen of the past.

HILL:

In other words, our overabundance has made us indolent and indifferent. Is that the idea?

CARNEGIE:

Yes, it has become so easy for a man to get everything he

wants in this country that the pioneering spirit and the will for self-determination have been weakened. There is danger associated with unearned gifts. The gifts of personal liberty and the right to free enterprise, which were provided by the founders of this nation, have come so easily that the people have begun to mistake their privileges for their license to expect something for nothing.

HILL:

From your remarks, I draw the conclusion that Uncle Sam's gift of overabundance, in the form of personal liberty as provided by the Constitution of the United States, sometimes produces the effect of causing his nieces and nephews to look to rich old Uncle for what they want instead of producing it for themselves, by rendering useful service. Is that about the story?

CARNEGIE:

That's the story exactly! Of course, this trend will right itself in time, but not until the country is overtaken by some great national emergency that will teach the people the fallacy of expecting something for nothing. This may come in the form of a widespread depression, or it may come in the form of a war in which the people will be forced to join forces and fight once more for the privilege of liberty that was given to them when this nation was born. But come what may, there is one thing certain: People cannot go on forever cutting down the amount of service they render and demanding more pay, without catastrophe overtaking them.

HILL:

Then you do not think there is anything wrong with the American system of economics, but there is something radically wrong with the people who are living under it? Is that your viewpoint, Mr. Carnegie?

CARNEGIE:

That is not merely my viewpoint, but it is the truth! It is little wonder that we have such a comparatively few men with Creative Vision, in view of the overwhelming number of people who are violating every rule of Creative Vision. There is nothing wrong with our system of government, or our economic system; but there is definitely something wrong in the use we are making of these privileges.

> THE mind within itself can make a Heaven of Hell, a Hell of Heaven. —John Milton

HILL:

Mr. Carnegie, you are the recognised leader in the steel industry. Your achievements in this industry have so far outstripped all others that there is no room for comparison. You have reduced the price of steel from $130 per ton to around $20 per ton. You have made the steel industry the very back-bone of American industry. Now, will you tell me how you happened to advance so far ahead of all others engaged in that industry?

CARNEGIE:

You have the answer to that question in the ten factors of Creative Vision which I have mentioned.

HILL:

Do you mean that you have observed and applied these principles while some of the other engaged in the steel industry have not?

CARNEGIE:

Oh, I would not put it just that way. I would rather say that I have applied these principles more persistently than have many of the others. The difference between my achievements and the achievements of others in the steel industry has been due largely to the difference in the application of principles.

HILL:

Then you do not claim to have greater ability than the others, just a greater capacity for the application of sound principles? Is that the idea?

CARNEGIE:

Yes, that is it. And I may add that this same difference, in the matter of application of principles, is the major difference between those who succeed and those who fail in other walks of life. The principles of successful achievement are as definite as are the rules of mathematics. Some men acquire an understanding of these rules and apply them persistently. Others may understand them, but they apply them with less persistence. Naturally, the more persistent a man is, the greater is the success.

HILL:

Mr. Carnegie, I have always been interested in understanding more about the transition by which one changes from poverty to riches. Practically, every man of great wealth in the United States appears to have started at scratch, with nothing but a sound mind and an opportunity such as every man has, under the American way of life. Now, what I would like to know is this: What is the first move a man makes when he is through with poverty and has become determined he will have riches? Where is the precise point at which the transition from poverty takes place, and how may one reach that point?

CARNEGIE:

Your questions cover enough ground to keep me busy talking for a solid month, but I will do my best to answer. To begin with, let me answer you categorically by reminding you that it is the burden of the entire philosophy of individual achievement to provide the answer to all your questions. However, I will be more specific and give you at least a starting point from which you may arrive at your own answers.

In the first place, a man must have the necessary Creative Vision to enable him to recognise the particular opportunity for which he is best suited, considering the amount of riches he desires and the kind of service he has to offer in return for the riches. That surely is the first thing to be considered.

Next, it is a well-known fact that everyone wishes for riches, but generally the wishes contemplate something for nothing, or something greater than the value of that which is to be given in return for it. The second step, then, is to kill off this fallacy by recognising the truth that there is no such reality as something for nothing, or something for less than its true value.

HILL:

I see, by the way you are starting off, that the question of change from poverty to riches is one of organised preparation. Is that what you are driving at, Mr. Carnegie?

CARNEGIE:

Now you have the idea, exactly! Riches do not come from

wishing. They come from a more substantial source, the nature of which I shall try to make clear. And I may as well add there are no known shortcuts to riches. While the road to riches is well marked, it is rather long, and at places, the going is a bit hard. These hard spots claim millions of victims who begin the journey, mainly because when the going becomes hard, most people give up and turn back or drop out of the race entirely.

Now, let us get on with my answer to your questions.

The man who prepares himself to change from poverty to riches is something like the farmer who wishes to convert a forest into a productive field. He first clears away the timber and debris. Then he plows the ground and conditions the soil. After that, he plants the seed. But all these steps have to be taken intelligently, and at the right season of the year, or no crop will be realised.

It is precisely the same procedure with the man who makes up his mind to be done with poverty. He must first clear his mind of all negatives and self-imposed limitations.

Then he must take inventory of his education, experience, natural aptitudes, and general ability, to see what he has to offer. After this, he must look for a market for whatever service he is capable of rendering. Here enters one of the more important of the principles of individual achievement, the principle of Going the Extra Mile. I have never heard of anyone changing from poverty to riches without applying this principle, and doing it as a matter of habit.

Up to this point, the preparation has consisted, mainly, of the clearing away of the obstacles that stand between men and success. The next step is that of making one's self success conscious: Riches have a way of gravitating towards the man who has made up his mind to have them. Indolence, indifference, self-imposed limitations, fear, and discouragement will never attract riches!

After a man has attracted favourable attention to himself, by the habit of Going the Extra Mile, he is then in a position to adopt a Definite Major Purpose and to begin expressing it in action, through a definite plan. His major purpose naturally will be based upon the sort of service he has for sale.

From this point on, he applies the principles of individual achievement in whatever combinations, and under whatever circumstances, his major purpose requires. But, mind you, he does not quit when the going becomes hard. If he has properly charged his mind with success consciousness, he will not want to quit. This preparation is an absolute essential for the acquisition of riches.

Here let me offer the warning that the man whose only object is to acquire riches will more than likely meet with disappointment. The best of all mental attitudes in which to begin the transition from poverty to riches is that in which a man centres his thoughts more upon the service he renders than upon the riches he is seeking.

Riches which are sought merely for the sake of the riches alone have many forms of evasiveness by which they avoid capture! Alas, I fear there are too few who recognise this truth. I sincerely believe that the best way for a man to accumulate riches is by making himself indispensable, through some form of useful service. All my experience confirms this. All that I have learned from the experiences of other men supports this thought.

HILL:

Then it is not possible for a man to accumulate riches by shortcuts or by joining with others who, by the force of numbers, demand more than the value of the services they render?

CARNEGIE:

Oh, yes, men can and do sometimes take shortcuts to riches, but their chances of success are so remote that this method is highly hazardous. Not infrequently does it lead to prison, and sometimes to a worse fate. Those who 'get by' – and the number is comparatively small – find that their gains are not permanent. They have a way of melting like the snow under a blazing sun. Ill-gotten gain is always a bad bargain.

Men who gain some temporary advantage by the sheer force of numbers may demand and receive, for a time, more than the fair value of their services; but they are like the man who killed the goose that laid the golden egg. The market for their services plays out, sometimes because the purchaser becomes bankrupt, sometimes because he flatly refuses to be cheated. Cheating, no matter in what form or under what disguise it is carried on, comes back on the cheater like a boomerang, to embarrass him. That is why, the Applied Golden Rule is, of necessity, one of the principles of individual achievement.

All this may sound like a preachment, but remember that it is also sound philosophy! It is the sum and the substance of the experiences of men who have tried all methods of accumulating riches. Fortunate, indeed, will be the man who accepts it as sound without having to learn this truth form trying its opposite.

HILL:

What is the most important requirement of men who aspire to accumulate riches, providing you can boil the answer down to one thing that is more important than all others?

CARNEGIE:

I can do that easily! The most important thing is ability to negotiate with other with a minimum of friction, so as to gain a maximum of friendly cooperation. This is simply another way of saying the most important thing in life is "human relationships". All success and all failure are the result of human relationships. The man who learns how to negotiate with others so as to gain their confidence and friendly cooperation has gone nine-tenths of the way towards success. From there on, the journey will be both definite and comparatively easy. In this attainment, the golden rule and the principle of the extra mile are vitally important.

HILL:

Do you know of any sound argument against any principle described in this philosophy?

CARNEGIE:

Now, if you hadn't included that word 'sound' in your question, I would have been compelled to answer in the affirmative; but, answering your question just as you stated it, I am compelled to say 'no'. The only argument anyone is apt to raise, in connection with the philosophy, is that which may be raised by those who want something for nothing, or those who would like to find fault with men who have succeeded, because of envy. I might include, also, those who would like to destroy the American way of life.

With these exceptions, you will find no one who can or will be likely to try to question the soundness of this philosophy. As a matter of fact, it is so obviously sound that it defies challenge by all except those whom I have mentioned.

HILL:

Now let us go back to your definition of Creative Vision, Mr. Carnegie. I wish to make sure that I understand the full meaning of this principle, and I also wish the fullest understanding of its application in the practical affairs of daily life. Therefore, will you analyse this principle more fully?

CARNEGIE:

Inasmuch as I have already described what the principle is, and what one may accomplish by its application, perhaps it would be well if I now tell you what it is not.

I can think of no better illustration of the lack of Creative Vision than that exemplified by an acquaintance of mine who was asked to invest $5,000 in Henry Ford's automobile industry at the beginning, when Mr. Ford was badly in need of working capital.

This man had the money, and he wanted to invest it. He consulted me about the possibilities of an investment in the Ford industry, and I strongly urged him to go ahead and put his money in. Several months later, I asked him if he had followed my advice, and he said he had not.

"In the first place," said he, 'this automobile is a new fad and it will soon play out.'

Now, that was mistake number one, which showed lack of vision.

"And in the second place," he exclaimed, 'I don't believe this man Ford knows what he is about.'

That was mistake number two, which showed that he lacked vision.

"And in the third place," he wailed, 'if I put my money in that business I have no security for it, because the business has nothing but an idea.'

That was mistake number three, which showed his lack of vision, because men of vision recognise sound ideas as being among the safest and the most valuable of all assets.

About the same time that my acquaintance had an opportunity to invest his money with Henry Ford, another man by the name of James Couzens came along with $5,000 plus a keen sense of creative imagination. He not only invested his money in the Ford Enterprise, but gave the business his personal services as well. He is still with the business, and while I do not know how much his interest in the business is worth, it would be my guess that it is no less than twenty times his original investment if not much more.

You see, James Couzens understood the value of ideas. He also saw a future in the automobile business, and, of course, I hardly need to mention that he saw that Henry Ford 'knew what he was about'.

[Author's note: Many years after this statement by Andrew Carnegie, James Couzens left the Ford business, and I have heard from reliable sources that he realised $12,000,000 from his interest in the business, not to mention the amounts he received, from salary and his investment, while he was in the business.]

HILL:

Going back, for the moment, to your story of Dr. Harper, of the University of Chicago. Would you say that he applied all ten of the principles of Creative Vision?

CARNEGIE:

Well, you analyse the cleverness with which he managed to procure a million-dollar endowment in a fraction of an hour from a man whom he had never met before, and you will have your answer.

However, I knew Dr. Harper quite well. Therefore, I am in a position to tell you definitely that he made it his business to apply the principles of Creative Vision in practically everything he did. He was known far and near as the ablest money raiser in the educational field.

Now let me cite you another example of a man who had Creative Vision plus. His name is Hugh Chalmers, who is now the head of a large automobile plant in Detroit.

When Mr. Chalmers was the general sales manager of the National Cash Register Company, his company became embroiled in a controversy with its competitors which brought it near the brink of failure. Business was falling off at an alarming rate. The salesmen in the field were sending pessimistic reports of their inability to procure business, although Mr. Chalmers knew well enough that there was plenty of business to be had.

Being a man of Creative Vision, he diagnosed the case, determined the cause of the decline in business, and laid a plan to remedy the evil. If you will observe men who have Creative Vision, you will learn that they do not quit when the going becomes hard. Instead, they generally put on more steam and gird themselves for battle, no matter what the difficulty may be. Well, Mr. Chalmers was like that.

Having formulated a definite plan for the solution of his problem, Mr. Chalmers telegraphed every salesman in the field to report at the general office, in Dayton, Ohio, for a conference. After they had arrived, he called a meeting in the company auditorium. The meeting was called to order. Then Mr. Chalmers arose and addressed the salesmen as follows:

"Gentlemen, I suppose you are wondering why we sent you a hurry-up call to come in. Well, I'll come straight to the point and satisfy your curiosity. For several months, you have been bombarding me with all sorts of pessimistic excuses for your failure to send in orders. Some of you give one excuse for the decline in orders, and some of you give another; but there is one thing on which you all seem to agree, and that is the fact that something is wrong in the field which makes it difficult for you to procure orders.

"Now I am going to tell you what the real trouble is. Our competitors have circulated the report that we are about to fail, and you gentlemen have picked up the backwash of that report and built it into a fear complex. There is plenty of business in the field, but you have sold yourself a bill of fear instead of selling National Cash Registers. I can tell you, here and now, that unless you throw off that fear and go back to work, you will have something real to fear, because all of you will be looking for new jobs.

"This is my analysis of the case, but I am not going to force it on you without giving you an opportunity to speak for yourselves. You go ahead, now, and tell me, in your own words, what you think the trouble is."

Having thus frankly stated his case, Chalmers then opened the meeting for a free discussion in which every salesman present was invited to participate.

The first man arose and began to unburden himself.

"I can't speak for the other salesmen," he began, "but I can speak for myself. All I know is that something has happened which has taken away my courage. Moreover, I find all the merchants hostile to our company the moment I announce my business and connection. In addition to this, the crops have been a failure in my territory and I don't think the merchants would buy cash registers, not even if they liked our company." With that little bit of expressed pessimism, the salesman sat down. Then another arose and began to relieve himself of his burdens.

"I can endorse everything that has just been said," he began, "and I can go much stronger. Why, do you know that in my territory, which is cattle country, the price of cattle has declined until it has disturbed the whole community? Also this is a presidential election year and everyone is waiting to see who is going to win before buying anything. And, in addition to this—"

He got no further with his remarks. At this point, Hugh Chalmers jumped upon the top of a table, held up his hands for silence, and exclaimed: "I want someone to get up and tell me what is right about his territory. Get your minds off what you think is wrong, for the moment, and go right ahead and give me some encouraging news. I know you can if you will be honest and tell the truth, even though you have to make embarrassing admissions to do it."

The next salesman arose, and this is what he said:

"Mr. Chalmers, I see the point exactly! I, too, came in here prepared to spill an earful of excuses, but the truth is I have not been working in the right mental attitude. I cannot speak for anyone but myself, but I can promise you this: I am going back into my territory and guarantee to send in orders instead of excuses."

He sat down, and the next man sprang to his feet. Said he: "Yes, and I can go the last speaker one better. I'm going back to my territory in a different spirit, and I'll guarantee to send in double the amount of business I have ever produced from that territory in the past."

As he sat down, another man jumped up and exclaimed: "Me, too, and I wish to say that I think we should all apologise for the trouble we have caused you by having to call us in here for this much-deserved spanking. I'm going back with a firm determination to double my business. If I fail, you may consider my resignation."

Then one after another arose and made similar speeches. Two hours later, the meeting broke up, and the men began starting for their territories. The following month the company's business increased to double the amount of any previous months. And I have heard it said that this dramatic procedure of a man with Creative Vision saved the National Cash Register Company from financial disaster.

Thus, the story goes, wherever you find a man with Creative Vision. These fellows know no such word as 'impossible'. They convert stumbling blocks into stepping-stones. Like Luther Burbank, they make two blades of grass grow where one grew before.

Men of vision dam great rivers and warm the hearts of a happy citizenry who can read their favourite books after working hours with illumination as ample as the noonday sun. They press a button at sundown and lo! the sun rises again.

In like manner, pioneer minds touch a spring on a machine and it begins to talk.

These pioneers spread a network of railroads across a desert, and the land yields golden grain sufficient to feed the nation.

They tinker with a few wheels and odd pieces of metal, and convert them into a horseless buggy that runs under its own power.

They place a few pieces of tin in a small receiver, connect electric power to it, and lo! it carries the sound of the human voice across the continent. Accordingly, friends in distant cities converse as neighbours do.

They build telegraph and cable lines across oceans and continents, and business between the far corners of the earth is transacted in a few moments for the service of customers throughout a troubled world.

They build transportation facilities and great retail stores, and the world's markets are brought to the front door of every man.

Men of vision send an army of workers to Panama, guide their labour, and cut two continents in half, thus saving thousands of miles and millions of dollars for shipping.

These men of vision rig up a few pieces of bamboo, cover them with cloth, attach a small gasoline engine for power, and the thing takes to the air like a bird.

Likewise, men with ideas begin with eighteen dollars' worth of watches, offer them for sale to a few friends, and evolve from that humble beginning America's largest mail order house.

Similarly, forward-looking men fearlessly sign their names to a document which they know full well may become their death warrant, and by their courage, they give liberty and freedom to the world's greatest nation These great spirits place their pen to a proclamation, sign their name, and give freedom to an enslaved race.

Men of vision insert a piece of glass into a small tube, turn it towards the heavens, and reveal worlds the human eye had never seen before.

They embark upon an uncharted ocean, in frail sailing vessels little more seaworthy than a rowboat, and keep on until they discover a new world.

They harness the waves of the ocean and convert their power into electrical energy that turns the wheels of industry.

They write an essay called 'Compensation' and reveal to the whole world the impossibility of trying to get something for nothing.

Forward-looking men fill bottles with a pleasing, brown-coloured drink, name it Coca-Cola, cheer millions of hearts, and quench the thirst of the world, to say nothing of piling up fortunes for those who distribute the drink.

Other men of vision preach a simple precept known as the Sermon on the Mount and set the whole world an example in human relationship worthy of emulation.

They foretell the future by looking backward into the past. Men with ideas write books that lift their fellows out of the depths of despair and give them a new start in life.

Pioneer minds combine the metals of the earth into alloys that resist rust and serve man in a thousand useful ways.

They span the widest rivers with bridges that hang from steel wires.

In fact, these men of creative vision provide the humblest citizen in America with luxuries which kings and potentates of bygone ages never knew.

Verily, there is nothing impossible for the man with Creative Vision! He is the forerunner of civilisation, the inspirer of individual initiative, the protector of human freedom.

So, the story goes, on and on, ad infinitum! Wherever men with Creative Vision are found, one also finds progress, prosperity, and high standards of living.

You wanted to know more about the principle of Creative Vision? Very well, look wherever you find a prosperous business, and you will come upon some individual who has this ability. It may be a man hidden in the background. He may be one of whom the public hears little or nothing, but he will be there just the same. He has to be, or else there would be no successful business.

And I can tell you something else that all the people of the United States ought to know. When we stop encouraging men to use Creative Vision, we may as well close up American industry and go home, provided we have any homes to go to. Men of Creative Vision are responsible for every factory, and for every job in every factory. They are also responsible for the American way of life as we know it today.

HILL:

From your analysis of Creative Vision, I conclude that you

believe this faculty, generally speaking, is developed as the result of some definite motive which stimulates the imagination to obsessional proportions.

CARNEGIE:

That's the idea in a nutshell! But there is something else I wish to say concerning this question of motive, and it is this: Instead of rewarding men of Creative Vision with epithets and brickbats, they should be rewarded with appropriate honorariums appropriated from the public funds; not as a means of paying them for their services, but as an acknowledgement of the benefits they bring to mankind.

The United States government should set up annual awards, to be given as honorariums to those who, in each field of industry, make the greatest contribution to industry as a whole and to the general welfare through their Creative Vision.

The same plan should be followed with reference to the professions and trades, and business and finance!

The honorarium should be substantial, on the order of the Nobel system of annual awards for outstanding achievements. Surely 'the richest and the freest' country of the world is big enough and farsighted enough to recognise, appropriately, those who, by their Creative Vision, have made and maintained the American way of life for the benefit of all the people.

I found the award system highly profitable in the steel industry; so very profitable, in fact, that my annual award to some of the leaders who worked with me amounted to over a million dollars!

Now, this is my idea of how to go about developing Creative Vision; not by using it as a shining mark at which men with radical tendencies are encouraged to shoot, but setting it up as a goal for which all men are encouraged to strive.

Individuals who are really smart will, of course, recognise the soundness of this suggestion, and adopt it for their own self-promotion. Those who are really smart have always done this. The employer who overlooks the possibilities of such a system of recognition for outstanding achievements among his associate workers is something like the ostrich that sticks its head in the sand when danger threatens.

HILL:

Your suggestion seems quite sound, Mr. Carnegie. The best evidence of its soundness is the fact that you have made it provide you with a huge fortune.

CARNEGIE:

Yes, if you mean by the word 'fortune' the knowledge I have gained from my relationships with men. The money I have accumulated is but a minor fraction of my real riches. Evidence of this may be found in the fact that I am giving my money away as fast as I can do so safely. The better portion of my riches consists of the knowledge which I am giving to the people through your cooperation. When your job will have been finished the people of America, and perhaps the people of the entire world, will recognise the truth that Creative Vision is the advance guard of civilisation, the foundation of all human progress, the major source of all riches.

I want the people to become wealthy, but my own experience teaches me that the greatest of all forms of wealth is practical wisdom through which men learn, once and for all time, that there is no such reality as something for nothing! That everything has its price, and the whole of the universe is so arranged that this price must be paid; that material riches, the same as all other forms of riches, are the result of personal initiative expressed through the principle of Going the Extra Mile.

The people of the United States are in need of a new philosophy. If they do not get it, the future of this nation is doomed to failure. No nation can thrive and grow without the leadership of men with Creative Vision. The people of this country are discouraging the development of this quality; they are placing penalties on personal initiative; they are forming themselves into groups and blocs which seek something for nothing; they are encouraging men to substitute crooked politics for profound statesmanship; they are permitting unscrupulous men to infiltrate themselves into public office and loot the public treasuries by their failure to exercise their right of franchise; they are substituting personal greed for public service; they are substituting Karl Marx for Thomas Jefferson and other great men of Creative Vision who gave them their privilege of free enterprise and personal initiative; they are supplanting the church with the politically controlled salon!

> WISDOM adorns riches and softens poverty.
>
> —Socrates

By recognising these signs of the times, I can foretell what is going to happen to 'the richest and the freest' nation of the world if the people do not undergo a renaissance that will lead them back to a recognition of the principles of human relationship which have been responsible for the Foundation Stones of Americanism. I can read the future by looking backward to the days of the Roman Empire, when the people destroyed themselves through the same weaknesses in which the people of the United States are now indulging. I do not need to be a prophet to foretell the future of the United States. I need only to read the history of the past, and to understand that history has a way of repeating itself.

HILL:

Mr. Carnegie, do you believe the people of the United States will have the common sense to recognise a sound philosophy of individual achievement when it is presented to them?

CARNEGIE:

If I didn't think so, I would not be spending my time coaching you to provide them with such a philosophy! Yes, I do believe the people of the United States have the capacity for an awakening. Of course, there will be no sweeping revival of sound thinking, but you will find a few men in almost every industry and every calling who will be smart enough to recognise and embrace the philosophy as a means of self-promotion. Through their example of successful application of the philosophy, it will catch the attention of others and spread, just as Christianity began, in the minds of a mere handful of men, and gradually spread until it is the greatest influence of civilisation.

Keep this one truth in mind: Sound principles, which obviously are of benefit to individuals for their self-promotion, will be recognised and appropriated whenever and wherever they are laid down by the side of unsound principles. Truth will stand out by the side of falsehood, like the shining sun in front of a blue background of space, wherever the two are placed side by side!

I believe the people of the United States will recognise and appropriate the philosophy of individual achievement because I know it to be sound. Mark these words and remember what I have said: Wherever you find a man who recognises the worth of this philosophy you will find, also, a man who has the inherent capacity for Creative Vision! Watch that man closely, and you will see him throw off the spirit of defeatism and take on a new lease of personal initiative. His imagination will become more alert. He will blossom out in unmistakable contrast with his associate workers. His friends will notice the change that has come over him, and they will speak of it. He will go ahead in his chosen calling, by leaps and bounds. His success will inspire others to inquire into its source. In this way will the philosophy of individual achievement gain a foothold and spread.

[Author's note: Experience with many thousands of people who have acquired a knowledge of this philosophy has provided unavoidable evidence of the soundness of Andrew Carnegie's prophecy as to the manner in which it would spread on its own merits. Already the philosophy has gained a foothold throughout the United States. It has been translated into the Portuguese language, for widespread distribution in Brazil. A special edition of it has been published in Australia, for distribution throughout the British Empire, and it has been translated into the major dialects of India, for special distribution throughout India. Negotiations are under way for its translation into the Spanish language, for distribution in all the Latin American countries. It has already been adopted in the public schools of the Philippine Islands and in many schools in the United States. Thus may one observe with what a keen sense of understanding did Andrew Carnegie prophesy that the philosophy might well become a leavening force in a troubled world.]

HILL:

How long do you think it will require, Mr. Carnegie, to

so popularise the philosophy in the United States that it will become the substitute for the radical philosophies which are now undermining the Foundation Stones of Americanism?

CARNEGIE:

No one could answer that question with any degree of certainty, but I can tell you this: The time required will be much shorter than the time you will have to spend in organising the philosophy. As I have already stated, you will have to spend no less than twenty years of research before the philosophy will be ready for widespread distribution. After your work is finished, there will be a period of seeming indifference towards your work, just as there has been a similar period of indifference towards the achievements of all men who have been in advance of their time. If the country should be overtaken by some great catastrophe, such as a nationwide depression, or a war that will upset the economic condition of the people, your big opportunity will come on the heels of that catastrophe, for the people will have learned that everyone must have sound rules by which to relate himself to others.

[Author's note: Again we have evidence, in abundance, of Mr. Carnegie's ability to foretell the future by looking into the past. This philosophy was begun in 1908 and completed and published, for the first time, in 1928, exactly twenty years in the making. Then came the nationwide depression which lasted many years. Already the demand for this philosophy has become so definite that it has been published in my book *Think and Grow Rich*, and now in seventeen Mental Dynamite lessons in a form which makes it of immediate use to all who have personal problems growing out of the disturbing condition of the world.]

□

Analysis of Chapter One

Mr. Carnegie has covered the subject of Creative Vision so completely that further analysis of the subject seems unnecessary. However, I shall briefly summarise the highlights of his analysis.

1. He clearly emphasised the difference between imagination and Creative Vision, by showing that one deals largely with localised circumstances while the other contemplates every factor which concerns an individual in his relationship with others.
2. He graphically presented examples describing both imagination and Creative Vision in connection with their practical application in the affairs of everyday life, thus revealing the technique through which successful men have applied these principles.
3. He emphasised the importance of the basic motives as the source of all personal initiative and also the source of stimulation of imagination and Creative Vision.
4. He specifically named the ten major characteristics of men who understand and apply the principle of Creative Vision.
5. He appropriately called attention to the fact that Creative Vision has been responsible for all human progress, in all ages and all countries.
6. He called attention, again and again, to the futility of the common practice of trying to get something for nothing.
7. He made an analysis of the future of America, based on the common tendency to demand something for

nothing, which should be impressed upon the mind of every citizen of this country, and must be heeded by all who expect to acquire riches in the future.

8. He called attention to the importance of acquiring the ability to recognise and to embrace opportunities favourable for self-promotion, and significantly mentioned that only those who become thus alert may hope to attain noteworthy success in any calling.
9. He gave a fine description of the procedure one must follow in with the transition from poverty to riches.
10. He emphasised the necessities of Going the Extra Mile, and appropriately mentioned the fact that he had never known of anyone attaining any station above mediocrity without following this habit.
11. He described 'human relationships' as the most important thing to be considered by those who aspire to noteworthy success in any calling.
12. Last, but not least in importance, he recommended that the people of the United States stop throwing brickbats at men with Creative Vision and start emulating them instead.

I come, now, to my own analysis of Creative Vision. It is based on the requirements of this changing world in which we live. Mr. Carnegie's analysis of this subject was made over thirty years ago. Since then the whole of civilisation has undergone and continues to undergo shocking changes which have made Creative Vision not only desirable, but absolutely necessary.

As I interpret the nature of the changes which are taking place in the United States today, there is one danger threatening every American citizen which outshadows all others.

It is the growing tendency to standstill, without protest, while one after another of the rights of free enterprise are, by one pretense or another, being removed!

As Mr. Carnegie has so appropriately mentioned, the greatest of all the privileges enjoyed by the American people is that of the right to exercise personal initiative without molestation. He called attention, time after time, to the fact that personal initiative is the basis of all achievements. Out of the richness of his own personal career, he drew picture after picture of circumstances through which men had succeeded by acting on their own initiative.

Creative Vision will be of little use to the man who is forced, either by law or by arbitrary regulatory rules, to limit the amount of service he renders.

It has been known, since the dawn of civilisation, that the service a man renders is cause and the pay he receives is effect, and that the latter is measured with precise relationship to the quality and the quantity of the former!

Just as a little fire produces a small amount of heat, and a large amount of fire produces a greater amount of heat, so does a poor quality and quantity of service produce poor pay, and fine quality and quantity of service produce a satisfactory amount of pay.

From this conclusion, there is no escape!

A long while ago, a great philosopher said: "The greatest evil of all people is that of refusing to face facts!"

The time has come when we all need to face facts and to recognise them for what they are.

The United States still is the land of 'opulence and opportunity'! We still have the Foundation Stones of Americanism intact, though they are being attacked and undermined from many angles.

We still have the right in this country to choose our own occupation, although some of us have been deprived of the privilege of making the most of this right.

We still have the right to vote and to elect to public office the men of our choice, although we have so abused this privilege by our failure to vote that it, too, has lost many of its benefits.

We may still belong to any church we please, and worship according to the dictates of our own belief, but through our indifference to the benefits of the church we have forced it into a steady decline in its influence for good.

We still have men with Creative Vision as the leaders of American industry (the backbone of our entire economic system), but we are showing our ingratitude by rewarding them with epithets and abuses.

We still have all the operating capital that is needed to carry on the vast industries of America, but we have shown such hostility to those who have risked their capital that they have become shy and suspicious to the point of refusing to invest their money.

Surely, this sort of indifference does not encourage the development of the Creative Vision that this country must have in order to remain the world's 'richest and freest' nation.

> THIS country now needs leaders of Creative Vision as it has never needed them before.

These are only a few of the evils which assail us! Let us face the facts and turn a bout-face before we lose the privileges of which we have so long boasted. As Mr. Carnegie has so appropriately mentioned, all individual initiative is based on motive. Let me see, therefore, what motive we can find that will justify the readers of this chapter in developing and using Creative Vision.

Suggested Fields of Opportunity for the Application of Creative Vision

Ideas are the beginning of all achievements. They are the seedlings of all progress. As a starter, let me mention a few ideas which I consider worthy of analysis and thought.

(a) There is a great need for a series of newspaper comic strips that will educate as well as entertain. Up to the present time, this need has been supplied, for the most part, by subject matter which is lacking in educational value. The 'comics' are the great national pastime for children. Therefore, they provide an unparalleled opportunity for men and women with ability to combine entertainment with education, plus the ability to do freehand drawing. Those who cannot draw pictures but have sound ideas might take advantage of this opportunity by forming a Master Mind alliance with those who can.

(b) In the field of radio, there is a similar opportunity for the introduction of radio programs which educate as well as entertain. Here, as in connection with the 'comic' strips, much of the program material is in need of elevation. Surely, there is enough 'Creative Vision' in the United States to save radio (perhaps the greatest of recent discoveries) from disintegration through the inferiority of its programs.

(c) There is a crying need for story books for children which will educate as well as entertain. The Creative Vision which rescues the 'comics' and the radio might well be turned to the production of books for children through which they may acquire useful knowledge as well as find entertainment. A recent examination of the available story books for children disclosed the astounding fact that this field is particularly lacking in books of the nature here described, and one prominent publisher of children's books enthusiastically expressed his hope that someone would provide him with the material for such books. Here, then, is an open opportunity for some clever man or woman who understands how to cater to children through pictures and stories.

(d) Some person who has yet found no outlet for his Creative Vision may make himself wealthy by inventing a method of adding to the services (and to the sources of revenue) of gasoline-filling stations which are to be found on the most prominent corners throughout America. These filling stations have extra parking space for automobiles; therefore, they are excellently located for the distribution of almost any sort of merchandise that people use. The man who finds a way to make use of this available opportunity will not only confer a lasting favour on those filling station operators who are barely making a living (and some of them are not doing that well), but he will find himself in possession of a veritable gold mine.

(e) There is a crying demand for Creative Vision in connection with the perfecting of safety devices to lower the hazards of automobile traffic. The high death rate from automobile accidents (over 36,000 annually) has created a need for a system of highways so designed as to lessen the chances of accidents. Perhaps this is an opportunity more suited to engineers than to laymen, but the person who creates any type of safety device, either for automobiles or in connection with the construction of highways, which will lower the percentage of automobile accidents will find a ready outlet for his talents. A signal system such as is used by the railroads may offer one approach to the partial solution of this problem. But the chances are that a road which is so constructed as to keep automobiles at a safe distance from one another when passing, and at road intersections, may come nearer serving the purpose.

There is also a great opportunity for the man who perfects a better type of material for road building; something that will not contract and expand with the change of weather conditions, with a surface that will prevent skidding in wet weather. Perhaps this is a field for the man with a knowledge of chemistry. It may be that a new type of brick, much larger and heavier than the ordinary building brick, and so constructed that the bricks are interlocking when laid, will serve the purpose. Some such brick might be manufactured from the waste from woodworking plants and sawmills, perhaps by mixing the waste wood with a composition that will resist water. When such a brick is perfected, it may also become popular for house construction as well.

(f) The millions of cubic feet of unused seating space in the automobiles that travel the public highways daily might be put to some practical use that would go a long way towards paying for the cost of operation of the automobiles. Someone who has Creative Vision may organise this wasted space into a new type of small package or express service that will become popular as well as profitable to all concerned.

(g) The educational system of America could stand modification in the direction of some sort of improvement that would inject more dynamic human interest and more substantial entertainment into education, thereby discouraging the popular game known as 'hooky'. Here is a great field for men and women with an understanding of pedagogy, plus a knowledge of the characteristics of the human mind which can be reached only by entertainment. The person who wishes to use Creative Vision in this field may also find a way of projecting his ideas into the field of radio, through some sort of school of the air, that will combine education and entertainment. The idea may be extended, also, to the talking picture field where education has already found an outlet but lacks the right sort of a system to make it universally effective.

(h) In the field of toys, there is, and there always will be, a demand for new and novel ideas that will appeal to children. Here, too, education might be combined with entertainment.

(i) There is also a growing need for constructive modification of the orthodox methods of church management which challenges men and women with Creative Vision. The churches need supplementary services in two directions. First, a system through which religion can be made more interesting, thus insuring against empty pews; and second, some form of service through which the churches may help to solve the daily problems of life more effectively as well as attend to the spiritual requirements of their parishioners.

The clergyman who contributes to the solution of these problems will make religion more usable and understandable, to say nothing of having the privilege of preaching to larger audiences. The need is so great and the opportunity so obvious that it should challenge the ablest in the clergy. Only a great religious renaissance can save the world from its own follies. But, let it be remembered by all who may wish to try their hand in this field, that any improvements that prove effective will have to be along the line of practical service aimed at helping people to live; not a service that overemphasises the fear of death.

Words alone will not suffice. What is needed is deeds! This old world is economically ill, and the illness affects every living person. Here, then, is an opportunity for the churches to intensify their influence by rendering more effective human service.

The program should be available to all who use it the services of a Master Mind group made up of skillful and experienced businessmen, bankers, lawyers, doctors, and others of community influence who are capable of assisting people in the solution of their daily problems. Such a group may be organised by any church, merely for the asking, provided the system is designed to render genuinely useful service, and not merely to talk. As regrettable as it may seem, preaching needs reinforcement. Every intelligent clergyman knows this, but not every clergyman knows what to do about it.

(j) Small businessmen and retail merchants are in need of counsel in order to meet the competition of the new and improved methods of merchandising. Here is a field for men and women capable of rehabilitating the present worn-out methods. Some are engaged in this profession already, but the number is small in comparison with the need. One such specialist works in cooperation with the electric power companies, confining himself entirely to the rearrangement of lighting systems so as to display merchandise to better advantage. Within one week, he made such improvements in one retail store that the store's business was increased more than 25 percent over its best previous month. This service should include rearrangement of stock, newly designed display counters, new window display equipment, and new and better advertising methods. The possibilities in this field are unlimited.

(k) Every printing plant that has modern equipment has an opportunity for someone who is skilled in the preparation of new ideas and practical plans for printing and advertising. Someone who has Creative Vision may enter this field and make himself so useful that very soon he will own and operate a printer's service syndicate through which he will supply printing ideas for a chain of printing establishments. One man wrote a brief essay titled 'What to Do with Boys and Girls', designed for use by business colleges, to be given away by them to the graduating classes of the high schools, and turned it over to a printer in Chicago. The last time he received a report of the sales, they had gone well beyond ten million copies, on every thousand of which the printer made $3. Figure out his profits for yourself! Anyone skilled in writing, or in creating ideas requiring printing for their practical use, will find this a profitable mill that will keep on grinding out profits.

(l) The soft drink field is a bottled bonanza! The person who puts his Creative Vision to work and produces a drink that will be as popular as Coca-Cola will be well on the road to wealth. The Coca-Cola business has made more people wealthy than any other soft drink in existence, but that does not mean that it cannot be equaled, or maybe excelled! The more soft drinks the public consumes, the less intoxicating beverages it will desire. So, here is a field that should challenge the person who believes that strong drink is injuring the youths of the land.

(m) The person who perfects a throwaway bottle that is strong enough to stand the pressure of carbonated drinks will be on the highway to riches. The bottle should be made of some such material as cellophane, so the contents will be visible. This may be an idea that requires the Master Mind alliance with a chemist for its perfection, but it has possibilities that are unlimited for the accumulation of riches. The bottle must be made cheaply enough to permit its being thrown away after the contents are consumed.

(n) Some clever woman, with Creative Vision, will make herself famous and richer than she needs to be by inventing some system of sewing for children that will teach the art of sewing as well as serve as entertainment. The patterns may be marketed through the five- and ten-cent stores, together with a course of instruction on sewing. The system should be arranged so as to interest girls in making clothes for their own use. The desire for pretty clothes, inherent in all girls, will serve to help put the idea across.

(o) The business of interesting prospective buyers of life insurance, automobiles, real estate, and other commodities, by telephone, will provide profitable employment for women with pleasing telephone voices plus Creative Vision. Contracts can be made with a great variety of merchants for the purchase of names of prospective buyers, and the work can be carried on from one's home.

And so the story goes on and on without end!

Some Who Have Found Themselves Through Creative Vision

The record of those who have found themselves through the inspirational influence of this philosophy is both extensive and phenomenal. They are to be found in almost every walk of life. If all their names were known and published, there would be no space left in this chapter for anything else. But I shall mention a few whose cases are typical of others. The seed of Creative Vision lies sleeping in brains where it is least expected, needing only an appropriate motive for its awakening. It exists in millions of brains whose owners live and struggle in penury and want, and will go back finally to the dust from whence they came without having discovered the riches they possessed.

Shortly after a one-volume interpretation of a portion of this philosophy was published in 1937, under the title *Think and Grow Rich,* a copy of it fell into the hands of a salesman for the Firestone Tire & Rubber Company. While he was reading the book, something in it, or maybe it was something back of the lines, touched off the spark of Creative Vision within his mind and started him on a new pathway to achievement.

Mind you, the book did not teach him anything he did not already know! It merely awakened something he already possessed, but did not know he had. But that was enough. Without asking for an appointment, he telegraphed the author of the book that he was coming for an interview. We met in New York City and talked for two hours. When the salesman took the train back to Indiana, where he lived, he took with him a different attitude from the one he brought with him to New York.

When he got back home, the town looked different from the way it looked when he left it. His friends looked different. His wife looked different. And they were different, because he himself had changed. He had come into possession of a giant amount of power that was destined soon to change his economic status.

The first thing he did was to follow the instructions laid down in this philosophy, through which he chose a new Definite Major Purpose. Then he followed through by creating a plan for the attainment of that purpose. He followed the instructions of the philosophy to the letter. His purpose was that of self-promotion into a bigger and better-paying job. An heir was on the way, and he needed more money. Thus, he had a definite motive for his choice of a new major purpose.

After his plan was completed, he took the train for Akron, Ohio to present it to his employer. He carried with him no feeling of fear or doubt. He knew before he started that his plan was sound and that it would work. That is a characteristic of those who awaken the Creative Vision that lies dormant within them. When he returned from Akron, his wife met him in the train. She saw his face at the window before the train came to a full stop, and she knew that he brought good news.

In his inside pocket was a new contract with his employer. It called for a position as manager of a branch office. You see, when a man takes possession of the Creative Vision within himself he becomes a center of attraction, a magnetised human being who attracts to himself what he wants!

And, if you should ask this man, he would tell you that it was as easy to sell himself into a managership as it was to sell automobile tyres to dealers. It was all a matter of what he himself desired.

As this chapter was being written, I received a letter from an insurance salesman explaining how he had discovered and used Creative Vision himself.

> THE most substantial progress is based on the long-range view.

The letter was brief. On the surface of it, there was no indication that any miracle had happened; but to me the letter told a story similar to those which are coming from all parts of the United States and from foreign countries.

I knew that a 'miracle' had happened! That is, that which had taken place inside the secret chambers of the salesman's mind constituted the nearest thing to a miracle of which I have any knowledge, for something had happened there which revealed to him the only sort of genius that any man possesses, that is the power of Creative Vision!

Briefly reviewing the outward appearance of his case, I see that this is what happened. He came into possession of a copy of the book already alluded to. Somewhere, as he read the book, he uncovered 'Aladdin's lamp' that called to him the genies which had been sleeping in his brain. Responding to its magic influence, he laid the book down, looked off into space, and began to ask himself questions.

'Why,' he began, "have I been spending my time selling small life insurance policies when I could just as well have so shaped my plans that I could sell large policies?

'Why,' he continued, "have I overlooked this something that I now feel urging me on to bigger and better things?"

"Why have I not lifted my sights and aimed at the stars instead of shooting at the dust beneath my feet?"

Then the answer came! It came in definite terms, and he knew that he was not the same man who had begun reading that book. No, he was a new man. He had a different attitude toward the world. He had a different attitude towards himself and the work he had chosen as a career.

He didn't stop by merely meditating! He recognised that a passive Faith is no Faith at all, so he began then and there to take possession of that strange power which had so recently revealed itself to him, and to express it in terms of action associated with his occupation.

Picking up the city directory, he began to run his finger down the column of names. Finally, he came to one that brought him to a stop. There was the name for which he was looking; it was the name of a man who was financially able to buy a large life insurance policy.

'Now,' he mused to himself, "why haven't I been to see this man before? Why have I been spending my time calling on men who could buy only small life insurance policies when I could have spent the same time calling on those who can buy large policies?"

Closing the directory, he arose from his seat, put on his hat and coat, and, without taking the time for further preparation, he went straight to the office of his newly chosen 'prospect'.

He was admitted with courtesy. He stated his business and discussed the details which life insurance salesmen usually have to talk about before they make a sale. In a little while he arose from his seat, shook hands with his new 'prospect', and thanked him for his courtesy.

As he walked back to his office, he carried with him an application for the largest life insurance policy ever sold in Des Moines, or in that part of the country. The application called for a two-million-dollar policy.

That is more insurance than most life insurance men sell in ten continuous years of hard effort!

Yet, he had not worked hard! In fact, it had not seemed that he had worked at all, the sale was made so easily. And that is another of the queer traits of Creative Vision. Those who use it get their work done with a minimum amount of hard work.

When he got back to his office he sat down and had a long visit with himself. He went back, in his memory, to the day he began selling life insurance and came up, step by step, over every inch of the journey. One by one he called back to his mind the people to whom he had talked who had refused to buy from him, and wondered where he had fallen short.

After he had reviewed in his mind all of his former interviews, he made another discovery so important in nature that it should become known to every man who is engaged in the business of selling life insurance.

He discovered that life insurance is sold to the life insurance salesman himself; sold before he ever calls upon his prospective buyer; sold by his own mental attitude, his own faith, his own conviction that every man should provide himself with this sort of economic security; sold through the power of his own Creative Vision!

And the beautiful part of this discovery is the fact that it placed this man in possession of an asset that will remain with him until he no longer needs it. No business depression can ever take it from him. The map of the world may be changed, and the people of the United States may perish through their own failure to look within their own minds for a power that can save them; but this man will never again become a slave to anything or anyone, because he has discovered the man within him – that other self – which cannot be enslaved.

This other self is known as Creative Vision!

The newspaper reporters heard of this 'miracle', and they besieged the salesman's office for a story. When they wrote the story, they neglected to mention the title of the book that had brought him to the most important turning point of his life, referring to it merely as a 'miracle book'.

When the story appeared, telephone calls began to come into the salesman's office. The wives of other men in Des Moines had read the story, and they wanted to know where they could get the book for their husbands. The bookstores were overrun with orders. Telegraph orders began to pour into the office of the publisher of the book, and that is how we learned what had happened.

The same thing is happening throughout the United States. This 'miracle' book, *Think and Grow Rich*, is helping to unlock the self-made prisons in which men have been confined because of their lack of recognition of the seed of Creative Vision within themselves.

About two years after the publication of the book that started these two men on a new highway to achievement, I presented an autographed copy to one of my friends in Atlanta, Georgia.

Six months went by and nothing was heard of the gift. Then one day I received a letter with which was enclosed a newspaper clipping telling the story of another 'miracle' the book had inspired.

And here are the details: Somewhere in the pages of the book, my friend made a discovery that he, too, was blessed by the power of Aladdin's lamp in the form of Creative Vision.

Like the other two persons mentioned above, he not only recognised the power of this book, but he proceeded at once to make use of it. When the discovery was first made, he was working in a cafeteria, at a salary of $45 a week.

One evening after his work had been finished, he put on his hat and coat and strolled down the street and began to put his Creative Vision to work in earnest. He counted the people who were passing that corner and made up his mind that it was a suitable location for a cafeteria. More important than this, he decided – mind you, the decision was his own; it was reached through his own initiative – that he would swap roles for himself and become the owner instead of the employee of a cafeteria to be located there.

But he did not stop merely by thinking; the next day he began to put his thoughts into action. By the end of the week he had rented a suitable space for his new business. Within three months he had finished decorating and furnishing the place with the latest restaurant equipment, and moved in and began business.

He did all this without one penny of money of his own. He did his financing by selling enough of that Creative Vision that had been asleep within him to a man with money who supplied the necessary operating capital in return for a half interest in the business. He paid for his own half interest with the experience he had gained in his former position, plus – and this is important – the use of his newly discovered Creative Vision that was so necessary in operating the business.

Within a year, the new cafeteria was out of the red and into the black to the tune of $1,000 a month. Thus, Creative Vision had begun to pay dividends in the first year of its use. What it pays in the future is yet to be determined. Already the alert manager has had many offers from men who wish him to open up branches of his business in other places. Opportunity has found him out, and it is dogging his footsteps, begging to serve him. And that is another characteristic of the man who uses his Creative Vision: He finds himself a human magnet and attracts favorable opportunities as an electric magnet attracts steel filings.

Today there still are worlds to conquer. Not all doors are closed to Creative Vision. The world eagerly awaits the man who originates, creates and executes the products of vision.

In the field of industrial chemistry, the scope is unlimited for creative vision. Agriculture pleads for men of Creative Vision, who will help the farmer to check the ravages of synthetic scientific products which are making such inroads upon farm products.

In textiles, aviation, education, food manufacturing, plastics and plywoods, cement and building materials, automobiles, coal tar products, rayons, radio, telephones, and in many other fields, the door is wide open for Creative Vision.

Someday some man or woman with creative vision will produce an airplane which can land without danger, or an automobile which uses little or no gasoline, or a home which will not burn, or a cure for the common cold.

Such an individual will be quickly rewarded, and may turn the world upside down.

The promise of America includes ample rewards for those who exemplify the spirit of hard work, of initiative, and of Creative Vision.

And you who are reading this chapter! What about you and your Creative Vision? What are you doing to arouse it and put it to work for you?

When and where and how are you going to search within your own mind for that power to convert ideas and aims and plans into the riches of life? It is the goal of this chapter to help you answer these questions! It is the purpose of the author to aid you in converting your share of the great American way of life into whatever form of riches you desire, but the first move must be yours! If you make that move, and it indicates that you are in earnest, I will offer suggestions that may help you with the second step.

Late, in 1909, I sat in my automobile, at Fort Myer, Virginia, and watched the Wright Brothers as they tried, in vain, to get their airplane off the ground.

An old man sat on the running board of the automobile, watching the attempt to get the machine into the air. Turning to me with a look of doubt on his face, this old man said, "Aw, shucks, they hain't a going to make that thing fly. If God had wanted man to fly, He would have given him wings to do it with." Now we know that the old gentleman was mistaken. God had not given Wilbur and Orville Wright wings as a part of their physical equipment, but He did give them Creative Vision with which they created wings and did fly, just as He has given vision to millions of others who are born, live a natural lifetime, and pass on without having come to an active realisation of their precious gift.

In the early part of the twentieth century, a young mechanic and his wife were busily engaged with a 'contraption' with which they were concerned. It consisted of a crude piece of pipe into which had been fitted a piston that moved in and out on a crankshaft. Working over the kitchen sink, the wife poured gasoline into that piece of pipe drop by drop, while her husband worked the piston up and down with one hand and pressed a button that sent an electric spark into the compressed air of the pipe with the other. Hour after hour, they worked without results. Then, finally, the gas exploded and the thing gave one kick which sent the piston outward. Mind you, it gave just one lone kick, but in that single stroke of a crudely built machine was the destiny of an industry which now gives employment, directly and indirectly, to no less than six million people. At the present moment, that huge industry is feverishly engaged in making some of the materials that will be needed to defend this nation against an insidious power that threatens to destroy the Creative Vision that founded the industry.

What about this 'genius' who founded the automobile industry in America? What ability does he possess which others do not have? You can boil it all down to one thing known as Creative Vision. But, Henry Ford has no more of this power than exists in millions of other minds. The difference is that he has discovered his power and has put it to work, while others have not!

Henry Ford did not stop by merely discovering that he could turn the wheels of a buggy with a crudely built gasoline engine. He kept on using his Creative Vision, adding one refinement after another to his original automobile, until today the modern product of his mind is about as perfect as a piece of machinery can be.

In every village, town and city of the United States, there is a potential Henry Ford walking around, perhaps without employment. Maybe he is complaining because of the lack of opportunity to get ahead. There are millions of such people who do not recognise that they are carrying around with them the seed of achievement which, if it were germinated and fed through action, would produce riches as great as those which Henry Ford earned.

How will these sleeping spirits be awakened? What stimulating force can be applied to their minds that will cause them to look within for the seed of Creative Vision which is the beginning and the end of all individual achievements?

This country needs Creative Vision now, as it never needed it before. The opportunity for the expression of personal initiative was never greater than it is now. The country has plenty of muscle power and brawn, but it is suffering with a shortage of brainpower! And the tragedy of this shortage is in the fact that it is brainpower that makes jobs for men who have only muscle power to sell.

There is no valid reason for any young man of high school age or over to be idle in the United States today; yet millions of youths of this age are making no move to make a future for themselves, although they know, or should know fully well, that today's leadership will be theirs tomorrow.

A little while ago, I sent out a call for a male secretary. Back came the report from the business colleges and the high schools that there was a shortage of male graduates for this sort of work. Upon inquiry, I discovered that the shortage is nationwide. Male stenographers are coming to be a thing of the past, although, as every well-informed businessman knows, there is no position in all industry which provides a young man with an opportunity for self-promotion equaling that of a secretary. Since the secretary becomes an understudy to the men who are managing industry, he has a chance to go to school under the trained faculties of the greatest of all schools, the 'University of Practical Experience', and to receive good pay for the privilege.

When you hear anyone asking "What about this generation of youths? What is going to happen to them when they go out to look for jobs?", I feel like shouting from the housetops that the answer to these questions lies within the minds of the youths themselves. Those who discover their dormant Creative Vision and put it to work will make jobs for themselves, just as others before them have done. The others will go on down the dusty road to failure, in the midst of an abundance of opportunities, just as this class always has done.

Two things are essential for the unfolding and use of Creative Vision. One is a willingness to work and the other is a definite motive sufficient to inspire one to Go the Extra Mile with the right mental attitude.

Search as you may, but you cannot find anything to take the place of these. Work and motive, by themselves, are not sufficient guarantees of enduring success.

What an interesting story we find when we dig into the achievements of a man like Henry Ford. He works; he has a definite motive behind his work; he Goes the Extra Mile, perhaps adding a few additional miles for good measure; but, fortunately for him, and the entire world, he is going forward, not backward. Instead of using his vision to rape the world as some selfish military conquerors have done, Mr. Ford is using it to put wheels under the era of progress in which he lives.

Anyone who masters this philosophy and learns to apply it will have much more power than any human being is capable of handling safely, unless, in his use of this power, he trims his sails in the direction of constructive service, as Henry Ford has done.

As I approach the end of this chapter, I offer a suggestion that is rich in possibilities for all who recognise its value and act upon it. The suggestion involves no great amount of time or effort to carry it out. I suggest that you lay the chapter aside, after you finish it, and take personal inventory of yourself.

> The creative vision of one generation develops into the laws and institutions of later generations of men.

Get away into some quiet spot, where you will not be interrupted for an hour, and have a visit with yourself, perhaps such as you have never had before.

First of all, find out what you would like most to do. Then lay out plans to begin doing it and begin, right where you are, to carry out your plans.

Second, recognise now and forever that whatever you get from life will depend upon what you give to life, through some form of useful service. Perhaps you may have some useful plan or idea with which you have done nothing. Bring it out into the open and place a description of it on paper.

In Wallace's story of Ben-Hur is the description of a scene that serves as an appropriate closing for this chapter. It had its settings in the ancient city of Antioch, when the Roman Empire was at the height of its splendor.

The rich and the idle had gathered to attend the chariot races. A wealthy man wanted to crown himself with glory by having his horses win. So, he called his slaves together and chose one from the group to become the driver, promising him that if he won the race, he would win with it his own freedom.

The races started. Around and around the arena, the drivers lashed the horses for their last bit of strength, but one of the drivers gained the lead from the very start and never lost it. In one hand, he held the reins, and in the other, he held the lash with which he drove the charging steeds for everything they had.

His mighty arms stood out like ropes of iron! Someone yelled from the grandstand, "Those arms! those arms! Where did you get them?" And he yelled back, 'At the galley's oar!' for he was the slave who had been promised his freedom for winning.

He had a motive, and the greatest of all motives at that, for the madness with which he drove his master's horses to victory. That motive was his desire for freedom.

Th Roman Empire crumbled and fell. The splendid city of Antioch has all but been forgotten, but still men fight on for personal freedom. Men do not rely on strong muscles now, as in the days of the ancients. Civilisation has lifted us to an understanding of a greater power. It is the power of Creative Vision, and its source is the brain, not the brawn.

With this thought, I leave this chapter with you. I sincerely hope that before you lay it aside, you will have taken inventory of your own mind, and that you will have found there both the seed of Creative Vision and an appropriate motive to influence its development through use.

Where there is no vision, the people perish.

The loss of money is unpleasant. The loss of confidence in self is fatal to achievement.

The combined wisdom and genius of mankind cannot conceive of an argument against the liberty of thought.

Think before acting, not afterwards.

□

Introduction to Chapter Two

Organised Thought

Andrew Carnegie's analysis of organised thinking has been presented at the end of this chapter for the reason that it is essential that a complete perspective of every factor that enters into thought should first be analysed. The first part of this chapter sets forth what I have learned about Organised Thought from Mr. Carnegie and other men I have interviewed.

The analysis of the first half of this chapter includes three charts in which have been presented every factor which is related to organised thinking. This is the first time that any attempt has been made to present a complete chart showing, in clear perspective, all departments of the mind, all the sources of thought stimulation, and the approximate relationship and importance of all departments of the mind.

Chart Number 1 is the key to the entire chapter, and it should be studied carefully before endeavouring to read the rest of the chapter. As a matter of fact, it would be helpful if the chart were enlarged, on a piece of paper at least eighteen inches square, and placed where it can be seen daily by the reader. The descriptive key to the chart, which appears on the page opposite to it, should likewise be copied in larger type.

Do not become confused because of the seeming complexity of this chart, for you will recognise, by the time you finish this lesson, that all departments of the mind have been so wisely coordinated that they operate harmoniously, and with less detail than is required to dial a number on a modern telephone.

Chart Number 2 sets forth the steps necessary to attainment of one's definite major purpose. Study it carefully, for it is essential to achieving success.

Chart Number 3 explains how thoughts are formed. All of the factors described in Chart Number 3 work so smoothly that they function automatically, in the performance of a part of their respective duties, and the whole system can be put into operation by the simple process of using the willpower.

I wish especially to call your attention to two important factors shown on this chart: the faculty of the will and the faculty of the emotions. These are the two departments of the mind which you must get under your control if you are ever to become an organised thinker. In every brain, there is an eternal conflict between the emotions and the power of will, and with a vast majority of people, the emotions get the better of the conflict. It is no mere figure of speech when we say that "the world is controlled by the emotions of men".

Now, the burden of this chapter is to enable the readers to reverse this rule so that they may truthfully say that their emotions are under the control of their willpower.

This chapter presents, from many angles, the means by which one may make the faculty of the will the real 'boss' of the other departments of the mind. Mr. Carnegie has gone into this angle of the lesson from the viewpoint of a practical business leader, but it will be clear from his analysis that he places the faculty of the will at the head of the list of important factors which determine one's success or failure in life.

In this chapter, you will come into a better understanding of that mystery of mysteries known as the power of thought.

It is no exaggeration to say that if you master this chapter you will have a philosophy sufficient, by itself, for the solution of practically every problem of life. Accurate thinking is the basis of all human achievements. I have presented a clear description of every major factor that enters into accurate thinking in this chapter. Do not become discouraged, therefore, if you do not master this chapter at the first reading.

And now a *few words as to how to read this chapter.*

As you read, be aware that the main object of the chapter is to inspire thought. Read with pencil in hand and mark every line that you may wish to emphasize. Read slowly and make sure that you understand every statement before you finish with it. And above all, think as you read. After you complete the chapter, lay it aside for a few days, then come back to it and read it again, and observe how much clearer it will be on the second reading.

Lastly, remember that an important part of this chapter has not been presented in these pages. It is the part that exists in your own mind, consisting of your experience, your ability, your education, and your thought habits. Add these to that which appears in this chapter and you will have enriched your own mind by immeasurable proportions.

Approach this chapter with the thought in mind that its sole purpose is to acquaint you with the functioning powers of your mind by describing how these functions can be controlled and directed to definite ends. It is hoped that through this chapter, you will be enabled to take possession of your own mind and use it effectively in managing all the circumstances of your life to your best advantage.

It would be surprising to me if anyone reads this chapter without experiencing a definite increase in self-reliance, willpower, and enthusiasm over the opportunities of life. It has been the experience of all to whom this lesson has been taught that they notice a complete change in their entire 'mental attitude', a change that practically eliminates fear, doubt, indecision and inaction. This chapter should have the effect of causing the reader to be born again and, through that new birth, discover the self, the self he did not know he possessed.

Yes, everyone has 'another self'. Housed in every person is a dual personality, a fact to which the psychologists and psychiatrists will testify. One personality is negative. It thrives on self-limitations, fear, doubt and worry. The other is positive. It feeds on faith, courage, definite belief in self, initiative, enthusiasm and the will to win.

So, join forces with me, will you, and let us combine our efforts to the end that we will kill off that negative personality which has been standing between you and the better things of life. This we can accomplish by feeding and encouraging the positive 'other self'.

□

CHAPTER TWO
Organised Thought

"Thoughts are things," said a great philosopher, and it is significant that thought is one of the few things an individual may control completely.

Thought 'magnetises' one's entire physical body, and attracts to one the outward, physical things which harmonise. The burden of this chapter is to show how the power of thought can be organised and directed towards definite ends.

This chapter is illustrated with three charts outlining, as simply as possible, the mechanism of the mind, and the sources of thought stimuli which start action in the mind.

Chart Number 1: Here is presented the route that must be taken in organising thought and expressing it in the attainment of a definite end. Observe that the starting point is desire, based upon one or more of the nine basic motives which inspire action. The stimulus needed to keep desire active is supplied by some combination of the known principles of individual achievement.

Chart Number 2: Here are shown the three steps which must be taken in the attainment of the object of one's Definite Major Purpose, together with the principles which must be combined and applied in the effective use of organised thought.

Chart Number 3: Here is shown the ten factors which constitute the 'mechanism' of thought, showing the sources of stimuli of thought. Observe that the subconscious mind is connected with all departments of the mind, and its source of power is Infinite Intelligence. Observe, also, that the memory, the five senses, and the emotions require constant self-discipline; that they are not reliable without the strictest of discipline; and that they need highly organised attention to bring them under control. This control is obtained by the exercise of the power of will, through the adoption of voluntary habits.

CHART NUMBER

DESIRE
THE STARTING POINT OF ALL ACHIEVEMENT BASED ON A COMBINATION OF

Attained Through Some Combination of The Seventeen Principles of Achievement

1. Definiteness of Purpose
2. The Mastermind Alliance
3. Attractive Personality
4. Applied Faith
5. Going the Extra Mile
6. Organised Endeavour
7. Applied Golden Rule
8. Inspired Feeling
9. Self-discipline
10. Organised Thought
11. Controlled Attention
12. Team Work
13. Liberty of Thought
14. Learning from Defeat
15. Creative Vision
16. Health Maintenance
17. Budgeting Time and Money

THE NINE BASIC MOTIVES

1. Emotion of LOVE
2. Emotion of SEX
3. Desire for HEALTH
4. Desire for SELF-PRESERVATION
5. Desire for FREEDOM OF BODY AND MIND
6. Desire for PERSONAL EXPRESSION AND FAME
7. Desire for PERPETUATION OF LIFE
8. Desire for REVENGE
9. Emotion of FEAR: based on seven basics fears: Fear of Poverty, Criticism, Ill Health, Loss of Love, Old Age, Loss of Liberty, Death

MAJOR PURPOSE IN LIFE – FINISHING POINT

CHART NUMBER 2

This Chart Shows the Order in Which Organised Thought Should Be Applied in the Attainment of Any Desired Purpose

DEFINITE MAJOR PURPOSE (First Step)

Can be attained through the factors listed below, in the order here shown. Proceeding according to this chart is, of itself, an efective form of Organised Thought.

Don't forget that your purpose should be founded on a definite motive, or some combination of the nine basic motives:

↓

PLAN OF ATTAINMENT (Second Step)

Success can be no greater than the plan is sound; therefore, enlist help in building plans.

↓

MASTERMIND ALLIANCE (Third Step)

Choose your "Mastermind" allies so as to procure experience and knowledge needed in carrying out your plan.

↓

THE FOLLOWING PRINCIPLES ARE NECESSARY IN PROCEEDING UNDER ORGANISED THOUGHT

1. Organised Thought
2. Applied Faith
3. Organised Endeavour
4. Creative Vision
5. Self-descipline
6. Going the Extra Mile
7. Attractive Personality

Study carefully the three important steps one must take, based on (1) definiteness of purpose (2) a sound plan, and (3) a Master Mind alliance with experienced helpers.

CHART NUMBER 3

Chart of the Ten Factors Which Constitute the 'Mechanism' of Thought. Observe That the Subconcious Section of the Mind Has Access to All Departments of the Mind, but Is Not Under the Control of Any.

INFINITE INTELLIGENCE
The source of all power of thought, all facts, all knowledge, available through the subconscious section of the mind only.

SUBCONSCIOUS SECTION OF THE MIND
The connecting link between the mind of man and infinite intelligence.

Below are shown all departments of the mind, with the three sources of thought stimuli at the bottom of the chart.

FACULTY OF WILLPOWER
"Boss of the mind"

FACULTY OF REASON
Master of all opinions and judgements

FACULTY OF EMOTIONS
The seat of most actions of the mind

FACULTY OF IMAGINATION
The builder of all plans

FACULTY OF CONSCIENCE
Moral guide of the mind

The three sources of thought which require the greatest amount of self-discipline are shown below.

INTUITION	THE FIVE SENSES	MEMORY
The "sixth sense" or intuitive knowledge.	1. Sight These become 2. Sound reliable only 3. Taste through strict 4. Smell self-discipline. 5. Touch	Storehouse of all thought and sense impressions. Filing cabinet of the brain.

KEY TO CHART NUMBER 3

1. Infinite Intelligence:

   The source of all power of thought, available through the subconscious mind only. Note that the chart shows all departments of the mind entirely encircled by Infinite Intelligence.

2. Subconscious Mind:

   The connecting link between the conscious mind and Infinite Intelligence. Not subject to self-discipline, but can be stimulated by the means described in this chapter.

3. Faculty of Willpower:

   'Boss' of all departments of the mind, with the power to modify, change or 'balance' the actions of all mental functions.

4. Faculty of Reason:

   'Presiding judge' that may, if it is permitted, pass judgment on all ideas, plans and desires; but its decisions can be set aside by the power of will, or offset by the influence of the emotions when the will does not assert itself.

5. Faculty of Emotions:

   The seat of most of the actions of the mind, the source of most of the thoughts released by the mind, and may be very dangerous if not modified by the faculty of reason, under the direction of the power of will.

6. Faculty of Imagination:

   The builder of all plans, ideas, and ways and means of attaining desired ends. Needs self-discipline and constant direction of the power of will to avoid exaggeration.

7. Faculty of Conscience:

   Moral guide of the mind whose chief function is that of modifying the individual's aims and purposes so they harmonise with moral laws.

8. Intuition:

   The 'sixth sense' by which one makes decisions based on subconscious information.

9. The Five Senses:

   The physical 'arms' of the brain through which it contacts the external world and acquires information. The senses are not reliable, and need constant discipline.

   Under any form of highly emotional activity, the senses become confused and highly undependable, as in the case of fear.

10. Memory:

   The 'filing cabinet' of the brain, wherein is stored all thought impulses, all experiences, and all sensations that reach the brain through the five physical senses. Also undependable, and needs self-discipline for perfection.

Some of the Known Facts Concerning the Nature of Thought

1. All thought (whether positive or negative, good or bad, accurate or inaccurate) tends to clothe itself in its physical equivalent, and it proceeds by inspiring one with ideas, plans, and means of attaining desired ends, through perfectly logical and natural media. After thought on a given subject becomes a habit, it is taken over by the subconscious mind and automatically acted upon, through the most available media. Everything is the tool of thought!

   It may not be literally true that 'thoughts are things', but it is true that thoughts create things, and the things they create are striking duplicates of the thoughts out of which they are fashioned.
2. Through the application of self-discipline thought can be influenced, controlled and directed through transmutation towards a desired end, by the development of voluntary habits suitable for the attainment of any given end.
3. The power of thought (with the aid of the subconscious mind) has control over every cell of the body,

encourages the cells in repair, stimulates their growth, influences all the organs of the body, helps them to function orderly, and assists in fighting disease through what is commonly called 'body resistance'. These functions are carried on automatically, but they may be stimulated by voluntary aid.

4. All of man's achievements begin in the form of thought, organised into plans, aims and purposes, and expressed in terms of action. All action is stimulated by one or more of the nine basic motives, as shown in Chart Number 1.
5. There are two sections of the mind that deal with thought, the conscious and the subconscious. The conscious section, operating through the five departments of the mind, is under the control of man. The subconscious section is under the control of Infinite Intelligence. (See Chart Number 3.) The 'sixth sense' is under the control of the subconscious section of the mind, and it functions automatically.
6. Both the subconscious and the conscious sections of the mind work in response to habits, adjusting themselves to whatever habits the individual may form, whether the habits are voluntary or involuntary. When habits are once formed, the mind proceeds to carry them out automatically, unless they are modified by other and stronger habits.
7. The majority of all thoughts acted upon by the mind are not necessarily accurate, being based on personal 'opinions', bias, prejudice, fear, and the result of emotional excitement in which the faculty of reason has been given little opportunity to modify them rationally. The five senses are so untrustworthy that they can be easily deceived, especially when they function under emotional excitement, such as fear, love, sex, or, in fact, any of the other emotions, without the 'balancing' influence of the faculty of reason.

8. The first step in accurate thinking is that of separating facts from mere indications or hearsay evidence.
9. The second step is that of separating facts (after they have been identified as such) into two classes, viz. important and unimportant. An important fact is any fact which can be used to help one attain the object of one's major purpose. All other facts are relatively unimportant. The average person spends his life dealing with 'inferences' based upon unreliable sources of information, and seldom comes within sight of that form of self-discipline which demands facts. Moreover, the average person never, during his entire lifetime, learns to distinguish the difference between 'important' and 'unimportant' facts, which may account for there being so many failures in the world. It is a matter of evaluation – putting first things first.
10. Desire, based on a definite motive, is the beginning of all voluntary thought action associated with individual achievement. The presence in the mind of an intense desire tends to stimulate the faculty of imagination with the purpose of creating ways and means of attaining the object of the desire. If the desire is persistently held in the mind through repetition of thought, it is picked up by the subconscious section of the mind and automatically carried out to its logical conclusion, by the most practical means available.
11. The known sources of stimulation of thought are:
    (a) The five physical senses (very unreliable).
    (b) The storehouse of the memory (also unreliable).
    (c) The subconscious mind, through which thought may be stimulated by the influence of Infinite Intelligence. It is believed by many that this is the source as 'geniuses', the assumption being that the person who, through self-discipline and practice, develops the ability to use his subconscious mind at will, thereby places himself in a position to

draw upon the power of Infinite Intelligence for guidance in carrying out his aims and purposes.

(d) The emotions, the seat of all desires. From this source comes all the thought stimulation based upon the major emotions, and inasmuch as these emotional feelings express themselves voluntarily it is necessary to gain control over them, through self-discipline. This is the source from which most of the thought stimulation arises, a fact which accounts for the saying that 'emotion rules the world'.

(e) Faculty of the will, the 'boss' of all other departments of the mind. Although this faculty is the 'boss' of the mind, it has been mentioned last for the reason that it is used the least, by the majority of people. By far the greater part of all thought stimulation of the average person comes from the emotions, and neither the faculty of reason nor the willpower is consulted in connection with most of these thoughts, an error which is responsible for so many mistakes in judgement of which the majority of people are guilty.

As far as is known, these five sources are the only sources of thought stimulation. Study them carefully (in Chart Number 3) and establish a clear picture in your mind of the factors you must deal with in order to acquire the ability to organise your thoughts. This chart should be consulted regularly until you understand it, for it is an actual 'picture' of the working equipment of all thinking. The chart cannot be mastered by a casual glance.

Begin your study of the chart by observing that Infinite Intelligence, the source of all power of thought, is placed at the top. Observe, also, that no faculty of the mind has direct connection with Infinite Intelligence; but all departments of the mind have access to it through the medium of the subconscious section of the mind.

You will notice that the first five departments of the mind (willpower, reason, emotions, imagination, and conscience) are connected separately with the subconscious section of the mind; also, they are connected directly with one another.

The three sources of thought stimulation at the bottom of the chart (intuition, the five senses and memory) have been separated from the other departments of the mind for the reason that they are the three sources of thought stimulation which are the least subject to the control of the will; therefore, they need special attention through strict self-discipline.

Three faculties of the mind (reason, imagination and conscience) perform definite functions in the process of thinking but apparently no thought stimulation comes from these. All three of these faculties modify thought after it is submitted to them but they do not originate thought. The faculty of reason compares all thought with one's past experience (as recalled from the memory) and forms all judgements and opinions. The faculty of the imagination shapes one's thoughts into ideas, plans, and ways and means of attaining desired ends. The conscience gives moral guidance to all thoughts. If consulted at all times, before one engages in expressing any thought in terms of action, these three faculties of the mind will become strong and dependable. If they are not consulted, and one forms the habit of acting on thought without their modifying influence, they will atrophy and become useless.

All faculties of the mind may be developed and made dependable in the same manner that one may develop a strong arm, namely by systematic use, through organised habits of thought. There is no other way to gain control over the mind except systematic use, under a plan that will give recognition to every department of the mind, according to the instructions outlined here.

Do not become discouraged if you do not grasp the complete plan of the operation of the mind the first time you read this chapter.

It is no easy matter to draw a picture of the operation of the mind so it can be understood at a glance. Read the chapter through; then lay it aside and do some thinking on your own account, coming back to the three charts to refresh your memory from time to time. If you master this chapter after a dozen such readings, you will be fortunate. Remember, however, that all the time you spend will be justified because you are here dealing with the most important force that affects your life – the subject of accurate thinking.

Let me here introduce another factor of great importance in organised thinking – one that has not been included in any charts. It is the importance of acquiring the necessary self-discipline to enable you to believe. For example, when you adopt a Definite Major Purpose you must focus all your emotional feeling on the object of that purpose, in a spirit of absolute belief in its attainment.

Let your daily slogan be 'You can do it if you believe you can!' By some strange power with which no one is familiar, the subconscious mind acts directly and immediately upon the thoughts which are based upon absolute belief, and proceeds to carry such thoughts out to their logical conclusion by practical and natural media which are available.

All great leaders are able believers! There are certain basic requirements of success in which one must believe in order to succeed. Some of them are:

(a) Belief in Infinite Intelligence (God).
(b) Belief in one's self.
(c) Belief in one's chosen associates.
(d) Belief in right over wrong; that right will prevail if one persists in believing in right.
(e) Belief in the proven laws and facts of science.
(f) Belief in the power of the mind to connect itself with Infinite Intelligence and become, therefore, irresistible.

Belief in these six subjects is a fundamental requirement of success. Accept them as such, and do not stop until you automatically believe in them all.

As strange as it may seem, the greatest power available to mankind is an intangible power, neither the nature nor the source of which is understood. It is man's only irresistible power, and there is but one way in which it can be appropriated and used in the practical affairs of daily life.

This power has given the world the best of everything that we enjoy in modern life. It has made the United States the richest and the freest country in the world. It has won every war in which this country has engaged. It has built the great system of railroads and the powerful industrial empire of America. It has uncovered a myriad of useful inventions. It has conquered the air and mastered the oceans. It has given us the power of instantaneous communication with nearly all parts of the earth. It has given us the highest standard of living known to civilisation.

Stated in one sentence, it is "the capacity of men to believe in something". Just that alone, without any modifying definitions; the simple, clearly demonstrable power of belief; the power that has worked miracles down through the ages. Not all the scientific knowledge known to mankind can cope with this intangible form of power. It baffles the minds of the shrewdest of men and defies analysis. It has nothing in common with logic or reason, and it overrides both at will. It is a law unto itself, and the strangest feature of this power is that it can be appropriated and used by the humblest person the same as by the most educated and renowned.

George Washington believed his little handful of soldiers could whip a vastly superior army and then they did it, although his achievement has remained one of the most baffling military triumphs of all times.

Edison believed that he could harness electric energy and make it serve as a light. He stood steadfastly behind that belief through more than ten thousand failures and lived to see his belief justified, although others before him had tried to accomplish the same result and failed – failed, perhaps, because they lacked the capacity for unshakable belief.

James J. Hill believed that he could bring the East and the West together with a great transcontinental railroad, and though he was only a humble telegraph operator, without money and with few influential friends, he translated his belief into a splendid reality.

The Wright Brothers believed they could build a machine that would carry a man safely through the air and backed that belief persistently through many heartbreaking failures until, at long last, they proved once more that even the law of gravitation is no match for the power of man's belief.

A humble farmer by the name of Mile C. Jones was stricken with paralysis, and the doctors told him he could never walk again. Fortunately, they did not tell him he never could use his mind again, for he took possession of that mind, began giving instructions to the members of his family, and lived to see his belief in one simple idea earn him more than a million dollars. That idea became known throughout America as 'Little Pig Sausage'.

Search the records of mankind wherever you will, go as far back as you please, and you will discover that the strong men, the great men, the successful men, have been those who believed in something.

The world belongs to men who believe! It always has and it always will. Therefore, in organising your mind power be sure to include in your plans a definite program of belief in the things you wish to become real. Let your belief be positive. Believe in something, not against something, remembering meanwhile that belief is contagious; that belief in one thing tends to open the way for belief in many things, while unbelief works in the same manner.

No one can rise above mediocrity unless he believes in his own ability to become and to remain self-determining. A student of this philosophy who had just discovered how to take possession of his own mind, through organisation of his mind power, expressed his gratitude for the new power revealed to him in these words:

I thank God for unwinding
The tangled skein of my life,
Thereby freeing my mind forever
From all forms of fear and strife.

Truly, the mind that has been brought under self-discipline, through proper organisation of the departments of the mind, may be 'forever free from all forms of fear and strife'. A disorganised mind can never be free. Mind organisation must begin with an inventory of the factors which enter into thinking, as they have been presented in Chart Number 3. These factors must be brought under self-discipline and directed to definite ends, through Organised Endeavour. The mind develops and becomes strong only through action. Even belief is useless unless it is followed by some sort of action appropriate to its nature and purpose. Passive belief produces no results whatsoever save failure and defeat.

When Henley wrote the following poem, he had in mind an active belief, although he did not make this fact quite clear in his lines:

Out of the night that covers me,
Black as the pit from pole to pole,
I thank whatever gods may be
For my unconquerable soul.
In the fell clutch of circumstance
I have not winced nor cried aloud.
Under the bludgeoning of chance
My head is bloody, but unbowed.
Beyond this place of wrath and tears
Looms but the Horror of the shade,
And yet the menace of the years
Finds, and shall find, me unafraid.
It matters not how strait the gate,
How charged with punishments the scroll,
I am the master of my fate:
I am the captain of my soul.

Yes, one may become the 'captain of his soul' if he will take possession of his own mind, organise it, and, walking "humbly before his God", express it in terms of Organised Endeavour, behind definiteness of purpose. What a pity Henley did not add one more stanza, making this fact clear.

And this is a privilege which the Creator left to every human being! To emphasise the great possibilities of this privilege, it was singled out and made the only privilege over which any human being has complete control. Men may lose all their worldly possessions, including sound health. They may be cheated, imposed upon, maligned, and slandered by others, or they may be unjustly thrown into prison and deprived of their physical liberty, but they still may think their own thoughts and use their own mind power without the consent of any other person.

How inconsistent it is that the only thing over which a human being has complete control is the one thing which most people make the least attempt to control. The inconsistency becomes all the more astounding when one recognises the fact that the power of organised thought offers the solution to all of one's problems, and nothing else does.

Test this statement by any circumstance of life you choose and observe how accurate it is. Whatever man desires, he may acquire with aid of his power of thought, provided he will organise his thoughts and apply his thought power in a spirit of belief in his own ability to make it serve his needs. Thought, applied in a spirit of belief, unlocks prison doors and gives men their freedom. It develops body resistance and frees men from disease where everything else fails. It supplants poverty with opulence. It dispels fear, worry, and discouragement and fills their places with hope, faith and peace of mind. Moreover, it works with the speed of lightning, requiring nothing but a determined will to put it into action.

General Instructions for Organised Thinking

Accurate thinking is based upon two important fundamentals, viz.:

(a) INDUCTIVE REASONING, based on the assumption of unknown facts, or hypotheses of facts.

(b) DEDUCTIVE REASONING, based on known facts, or what is believed to be facts.

As I expressed before, there are two major steps necessary in accurate thinking. First, one must separate facts from mere fiction, opinions, and hearsay evidence. Second, one must separate facts into two classes: important and unimportant. An important fact is any fact that can be used to advantage in the attainment of one's aims and purposes.

'Opinions', which form the basis of most so-called thinking, generally are not reliable, and often they may be very dangerous, because they are frequently based on bias, prejudice, intolerance, guesswork, hearsay evidence, or outright ignorance. The following facts concerning 'opinions' should be known to all who wish to learn how to think accurately:

(a) No opinion may be safely relied upon unless based upon known facts, or upon faith in the Divine Plan, and no one is entitled to express an opinion on any subject without reasonable assurance that it is founded on facts. Opinions are the freest thing in the world, and most of them are worth exactly what they cost – nothing!

(b) Free advice, volunteered by friends, relatives, and chance acquaintances, often is not worthy of consideration, and always should be scrutinised very carefully before being accepted as a reliable guide in thinking.

(c) Accurate thinkers permit no one to do their thinking for them. They ascertain the sources of such facts as they desire and make wise use of the sources for their guidance.

(d) Scandalmongers and gossipers are not reliable sources from which to procure facts on any subject, yet they wield a mighty influence in the lives of most people.

(e) Wishes often are the fathers to thoughts, and many people have a bad habit of assuming facts to harmonise with their wishes. In your own behalf, watch this common human weakness carefully.

(f) General information is abundant, and most of it is free, but facts have an elusive habit, and generally there is a price attached to them. The price is painstaking labour in examining them for accuracy.

Some Acid Tests to Be Made in Separating Facts from Mere Information or Inference

Scrutinise with great care everything you read in books, regardless of who wrote them, and never accept the conclusions of any writer as being conclusive without asking the following questions and satisfying yourself as to the correctness of the answers:

1. Is the writer a recognised authority on the subject on which he writes?
2. Did the writer have an ulterior or selfish motive other than that of imparting accurate information?
3. Is the writer a paid propagandist whose profession is that of organising public opinion for a price? If he is, weigh his conclusions with unusual care.
4. Has the writer a profit interest or other personal interest in the subject on which he writes? If so, make allowance for this in the acceptance of his conclusions.
5. Is the writer a person of sound judgement, and not a fanatic on the subject on which he writes? Fanatics are inclined to exaggerate, even when stating facts, and to colour facts so they may convey misleading impressions.
6. Are there reasonably accessible sources from which the writer's statements may be checked and verified? If so, consult them before accepting his conclusions.
7. Ascertain, also, the writer's reputation for truth and veracity. Some writers are careless concerning the truth.

   Half-truths are frequently the most dangerous truths.
8. Be careful about accepting as facts the statements of overzealous persons who have the habit of allowing their imaginations to run wild. Such people are known as 'radicals' and their conclusions may be misleading if relied upon.
9. Learn to be cautious and to use your own judgement, no matter who is trying to influence you. If a statement does not harmonise with your own reasoning power (and you should train your reason to function clearly), if it is out of harmony with your own experience, hold it up for further examination before accepting it as fact. Falsehood has a queer way of bringing with it some warning note, perhaps in the tone of one's voice, or in the expression on one's face, if it comes through the

spoken word. Train yourself to recognise this warning and to be guided by it.

10. In seeking facts from others, do not disclose to them what facts you expect to find, as many people have the bad habit of trying to please, even if they have to exaggerate or falsify in order to do so.
11. Science is the art of organising and classifying facts! When you wish to make sure you are dealing with facts, seek scientific sources for their testing wherever possible. Men of science usually have neither the motive nor the inclination to modify or change facts for any purpose whatsoever.
12. Your emotions are not always reliable, and generally they influence you to reach decisions regardless of facts. Before being influenced too far by your emotions, give your reasoning faculty (your 'head') a chance to pass judgement on the business at hand, whatever it may be. The head is always more dependable than the emotions (the 'heart'). The person who forgets this generally lives to regret his neglect.
13. These are some of the commonest enemies of sound thinking, and they should be scrutinised carefully before reaching decisions:
    (a) The emotions of love and sex. Either of these emotions may easily override facts and render the faculty of reason useless. Don't let them do it!
    (b) Hatred, anger, jealousy, fear, revenge, greed, vanity, egotism, procrastination, and the desire for something for nothing, usually known as the 'gambling instinct'. These emotions frequently distort facts.
    (c) Uncontrolled enthusiasm and imagination. Keep a close watch over these two, as they may be as dangerous as they are beneficial, because they are clever tools of self-deceit.

Let your mind be always an eternal question mark. Not in a sense of being a confirmed skeptic who believes in nothing, but as a cautious person who wishes to be accurate in his thinking. Question everything and everyone until you satisfy yourself that you are dealing with facts. Do this quietly, in the silence of your own mind, and avoid being known as a 'Doubting Thomas'. Be always a good listener, but also be an accurate thinker as you listen, when others are speaking.

Remember, you are living in an age when the distribution of propaganda has become a highly skilled profession. The most dangerous forms of propaganda are those whose sources of origin or whose purpose are not recognisable. In fact, if either the source or the purpose are obvious, the attempt to influence is not propaganda; it is plain advertising!

Remember, also, that you have been given three important fact-finding departments of the mind, namely: (1) the power of will, (2) the faculty of reason, and (3) the faculty of conscience. These departments of the mind become strong and reliable only through discipline, training, and use. Give them a chance to pass on everything you wish to accept as facts. Form the habit of relying upon their decisions. If you fail to do this, you may never be an accurate thinker.

Be very careful about accepting as facts anything that in these three areas of the mind: (1) the five senses, (2) the emotions, and (3) the memory. All three of these sources are faulty, and they require the strictest of self-discipline before they become dependable. Any practical psychologist can deceive you through all five of your physical senses, and you are doubtlessly deceiving yourself through these senses, almost daily. For example, if you cross the second finger of either hand over the first finger, and place a small object between the tips of the two fingers so that it touches both, your sense of touch will deceive you before your very eyes, by registering two objects instead of one. The moment you take your fingers out of their accustomed positions, and thereby interfere with their 'habits', they cease to inform you accurately. Similarly, all of the five senses may be deceived.

The emotions, likewise, can be easily deceived. For example, when one is submitted to fear, through any sort of an emergency which causes the emotion of fear to become stimulated, that emotion will deceive the sense of sight, or the sense of sound, or the sense of smell, or the sense of touch – a fact which has been established beyond any room for doubt. It is in response to false impressions of the emotions, or the five senses, that men and women become hypochondriacs (people who suffer with imaginary illness). The cure in such cases usually can be affected only by the psychiatrist, or the doctor who is skilled in suggestive therapeutics.

This discussion is intended to suggest to you that you should be cautious in accepting information received from others, but very cautious indeed in accepting the information you receive from yourself. It seems regrettable that one should be warned against the acceptance of information that originates in his own mind, but the warning is justified by the great number of people who go down to failure because they deceive themselves in their own thinking. The art of 'kidding yourself' is a dangerous one to use.

The mind is a queer piece of mechanism. It acts upon the impulses of thought, whether they are destructive or constructive, accurate or inaccurate, a truth which can be verified by the fact that the history of healing is filled with cases of people whose faulty thinking has actually produced the physical symptoms of disease when in reality there was no basis for the disease except that of thought.

If one's dominating thoughts are based upon the acceptance of poverty, the subconscious mind proceeds to carry out thoughts to their logical conclusion. The mind works in the same manner when one's dominating thoughts are of opulence and plenty. Gain control of your own mind, force it to feed upon thoughts of your own choosing, and you will then be in reality 'the master of your fate, the captain of your soul', as Henley expressed this thought in his poem.

Your Thinking Habits are the Result of Social and Physical Heredity

This chapter on organised thinking would not be complete without a brief description of two important laws of nature through which every human being is influenced or controlled.

One is known as the law of social heredity and the other as the law of physical heredity.

Through the law of physical heredity, one acquires all of one's physical traits, consisting of the genetic characteristics passed down by the generations of one's ancestors. This law provides us with a physical estate that is permanent and fixed as far as the body is concerned, and there is nothing we can do to change the hereditary factors of that estate. However, the Creator provided man with the means by which the physical inheritance may, to an extent, be overcome, guided, controlled, modified, and made to serve the individual according to his own ways of thinking, through what is known as the law of social heredity.

Stated in the simplest possible terms, social heredity consists of environmental influences, education, experience, and impulses of thought produced by external stimuli – especially those received through the following sources:

(a) Religious training.
(b) Educational training.
(c) Political and economic training.
(d) Social intercourse of every nature whatsoever.
(e) Tradition passed on from parents to children.
(f) Business, professional, and occupational habits and influences.

Here, then, are the six major environments which influence thought, and it is to these sources we must turn to get a clear understanding of why we think as we do. Through the operation of the law of social heredity most people acquire their ideas, beliefs, opinions, and thinking habits. We must understand this truth if we are to become accurate thinkers. We must face the fact that most of that which we express as our individual belief is but a reflection of the belief, or pretended belief, of those nearest to us. This is so true that any practical psychologist can make a surprisingly accurate analysis of the majority of people by studying their daily associates, knowing, as he does, that most people absorb the thought habits of those with whom they associate closely. Children are far more susceptible to the influence of social heredity than are adults, because their minds are open, alert, receptive, and not generally trained in the necessity of questioning the influences around them. It is this well-known fact which accounts for the statement, once made by the leader of a certain religious sect, that if he were given complete control of any child from the time of its birth until it reached the age of seven, he could so thoroughly instill his religious views in the child's mind that those views could never be removed.

Not all children, of course, are fully susceptible to such complete control and shaping of their minds on religion, or any other subject, but the majority of them are. Once in a great while, a child is born who, for reasons unknown to anyone, takes possession of its own mind and does its own thinking. When that happens, the world has found a potential free thinker; but the world never has many of this type at any given period. Most people do their thinking at second hand, so to speak, by merely reflecting the thoughts, ideas, and beliefs of those around them, and this applies to both children and adults.

We hardly need to call attention to the fact that this sort of thinking is not dependable, and seldom is it accurate, taking it as a whole.

We probably have more accurate thinkers in the United States than exist in any other country, regardless of the population or the nature of the system of living, and this for the reason that the American way of life provides the people with the greatest possible incentive for independent thinking. Contrast the American way of life with that existing in countries where the schools, the churches, the newspapers, the radio, and every other possible source of influence are under the strict control and censorship of the government!

In a country like Russia, or Germany, for example, the government can and does literally produce a race of people who believe that which those in control of the government wish them to believe. The people can do nothing else; at least the youths who come under the influence of the government propaganda machine from the date of their birth can do nothing else, because their thinking is made to order for them and forced upon them, through the law of social heredity. Their thought patterns are forced on them through their schooling, their religious training, their reading, and to a large extent through their social intercourse with the members of their own families and their neighbours.

If we placed all the leading contributing influences of social heredity under the control and direction of one man, here in the United States, that man could mould the minds of youths so that in one generation, he could enforce upon them any idea, belief, or purpose he chose. Here is the greatest of all the evils of a one-man government. It produces a nation of one-man thinkers, destroys the privilege of independent thought and personal initiative, and makes the people submissive and willing to accept whatever living conditions are imposed upon them.

If there is one tragedy greater than all others that can overtake an individual, it is that of being robbed at birth of his God-given right to take possession of his own mind and use it in his own way. The very fact that man was so created that he has control over but one thing, and that one thing is the right to direct his own thoughts, clearly signifies the Creator's purpose and plan to give mankind freedom through self-effort. It is not likely that the Creator ever intended that any human being should be enslaved by anyone, by being deprived of his privilege of thinking his own thoughts. The idea of using the law of social heredity to deprive people of the privilege of doing their own thinking is purely a man-made idea, and it is one of the most tragic abuses of natural law known to civilisation.

One of the greatest blessings of the American way of life consists in the marvelous public school system which, because of its decentralisation, makes it well-nigh impossible for one man or one group of men to fix any idea permanently in the minds of the youths of America by the control of the school system. In our country, the public schools are under the control of local citizens in each school community, and be it said to their everlasting credit that for the most part, the men and women on the boards of education, the school superintendents, the principals, and the teacher are American citizens whose character, integrity, loyalty to country, and judgement are of the highest order.

Under our school system, the youths are taught to respect the flag of the United States, but that is about the extent of any single idea that is imposed upon the youths of all the schools as a whole, and even that is not forced upon them; it is taught them by methods which permit them to use their own faculty of reason.

In the United States, all the major sources of thought inspiration, such as the newspapers, radio, schools and books, are so managed that every individual may accept or reject any idea that is passed on through these sources. Therefore, we have every opportunity in this country to become untrammeled thinkers, to use our minds as the Creator intended we should be permitted to use them.

If a person's thinking is faulty in this country, the fault is of the man's own making, and not imposed upon him by any system designed to pervert the law of social heredity to unworthy ends, as is done in many other countries.

Despite the great advantages of our system which encourages independent thought, the fact still remains that the majority of our people neglect their privilege of thinking for themselves, and become the victims, to a large degree, of the faulty thinking of those nearest to them. This is due, to a large extent, to the lack of understanding of the factors of social heredity. With all the many advantages of our public school system, it has failed to provide the youths of America with a clear understanding of the process of sound thinking, and it has taught them too little of the influences of social heredity, or the media which inspire most of their thinking. This obvious weakness has made it seem necessary for me to explain the law of social heredity as an essential part of the philosophy of individual achievement, as no one may become self-determining without a clear understanding of the sources of his own thoughts.

How We Acquire 'Opinions' Through the In□uence of Social Heredity

Most 'opinions' are not only valueless, but they are dangerous when they are not based on sound premises! Let us have a look at the sources from which many opinions come.

Most political alliances are based upon impressions one gets from association with relatives and friends, during youth. The late Bob Taylor (formerly Governor of Tennessee) once brought home to a young man, in a dramatic manner, the source from which he derived his political viewpoint. 'Why,' asked Governor Taylor, "are you such a confirmed Democrat?" Quick as a flash of lightning, the young man replied, saying, 'I am a Democrat because I live in Tennessee and my father and my grandfather were Democrats. That's why!' 'Well,' chuckled the jocular Governor, "wouldn't you be in a bad fix if your father and your grandfather had been horse thieves?"

It is doubtful whether one person out of every thousand who is allied with either of the two major political parties of this country could intelligently describe the difference between the two parties. Yet most people have very strong convictions that the political party to which they belong is the only party worthy of their support. Those who could explain the differences between these two parties probably could not give a satisfactory reason why the belong to their chosen party, nor would they suspect that their alliance may be the result of the influences to which they have been submitted since childhood, rather than sound reasoning as to the relative merits of the two parties.

In religion, one would find the same sort of condition. We suspect that there are only a few church members of any denomination who could clearly define the difference between the various religious denominations of the United States, and it may be no great exaggeration to say that the majority of those who belong to churches could not describe, accurately, the religious tenets of their own church, let alone those of other churches. Yet they have strong convictions that their church is the preferred one, little realising that their 'opinions' are the result of social heredity and not the outcome of carefully thought-out religious convictions.

Most people form the habit of embracing the beliefs of those with whom they associate most closely without regard to the soundness of their beliefs. The manner in which people come by their beliefs was aptly defined in four lines by Alexander Pope, who described how one develops criminal tendencies, viz.:

Vice is a monster of so frightful a mien,
As, to be hated, needs but to be seen;
Yet seen too oft, familiar with her face,
We first endure, then pity, then embrace.

And that is true of any idea we embrace. At first we may not accept the idea, but close association with it gradually influences us to endure it, then to embrace it as our own, often forgetting the actual source from whence it came.

The mind absorbs any idea to which it is repeatedly submitted, whether the idea be sound or unsound, right or wrong, and experienced criminologists tell us that nearly all youths who develop bad habits do so because of close association with other youths or adults who set the example.

The drinking habit, for example, became popular during the Prohibition era, when the sneaking of a drink from behind locked doors was looked upon as an act of 'smartness'. People who never took a drink of intoxicating liquor prior to the days of Prohibition developed the habit because "everybody was doing it."

In a like manner, the cigarette habit became the 'national pastime' for youths and adults alike. We have never yet heard of anyone beginning the habit without having to cultivate a taste for cigarettes, which shows clearly that the habit is not the result of a natural liking for cigarettes, but it is the result of the common tendency of people to imitate the things they see others doing, and this applies to thinking the same as to all other habits.

It is the rarest sort of experience to find any person, anywhere, at any time, who lives his own life, thinks his own thoughts, develops his own habits, and makes even the slightest attempt to be himself! Take a look at those whom you know best, study them carefully, and be convinced of this truth. Most people trail along, accepting and acting on the thoughts of others, very much in the same manner that sheep trail along after one another, over established paths in the pasture fields. Once in a great while, someone will pull away from the crowd, blaze his own trail of thought, form his own habits, think his own thoughts, and be himself, and when you find such a person, behold! you are face-to-face with a thinker.

In business, in the professions, in art and music and the trades, we find the majority of people trailing along after those who have gone before them, making not the slightest attempt to be original, or to think for themselves. The legal profession, for example, is largely influenced by precedent. They are so dependent upon precedent that judges render 'opinions' on the basis of what some judge before them has decided, and on such opinions are the merits of legal cases adjudicated. The doctors are almost as definitely bound by precedent as are the lawyers, both of which statements are readily admitted by physicians and lawyers.

The man who said that 'half of that which we believe is not true', stated the truth very modestly. He might well have increased the percentage, in some instances to where he might have said, 'Most that we believe is partly untrue,' without being very far wrong.

It is a rare experience to find a man who does not make the mistake of believing that because some statement appears in the newspapers it is true, and there are people who accept as truth the stories that appear in books, solely on the basis of the antiquity of the books!

It would be difficult to find a person who does not have an 'opinion' one way or another on Einstein's theory of relativity, although if you asked most of them to explain the theory, they would not be able to do so.

Another weakness of most people is the common habit of unbelief! When the Wright Brothers announced that they had built a machine that could be flown through the air, and asked the newspaper reporters to come out to their flying ground and see for themselves the newspapermen were so skeptical that they refused to go. The idea of a flying machine was new; therefore, no one believed in it except the two men who had created the machine. "Contempt prior to examination", as one philosopher expressed it, is a common fault in all thinking.

When Marconi announced that he could send a message through the ether, without the use of wires, his own relatives became so alarmed that they had him examined by a specialist, believing he had actually lost his reason. No one had ever sent a message in that manner before; therefore, the pseudo-thinkers 'reasoned' it could not be done. A similar experience has been the part of every man who has created something entirely new.

People simply must have 'precedents' by which to govern their thinking. It never seems to occur to them to examine the facts and get first-hand information. Those who do are the Thomas A. Edisons, the Henry Fords, the Alexander Graham Bells, and the other exceptions who have been the pioneers and the advanced guards of human progress; thinkers, all!

Controlled Habit, the Basis of Organised Thinking

Now let us combine the two important principles of habit and of social heredity and see what they will reveal. The law which forces upon every living thing the dominating influences of the environment in which it lives is a natural law, and it is difficult to change. This law works through what we call "social heredity"–influences we derive from social relationships. It is difficult to change. However, it can be used to great advantage by combining with it the principle of controlled habit! And let us remember that habit is something we can control.

Here, then, begins the story of organised thinking which I wish to present in terms so simple that any child who can read can understand. Read slowly and think as you read, for I am here approaching the analysis of one of the greatest of miracles – the miracle of creative thought – through which one may translate the impulses of thought into their physical or financial or spiritual equivalents.

If there is one portion of this philosophy which is more profound than any other, it is this portion which I am now presenting, for we are here dealing with the real power behind human achievements; the power that is responsible (through its misuse) for much human misery; the power that brings success or failure, according to the way it is applied.

Inasmuch as I am presenting a word picture of an intangible power, let me use a well-known simile through which to convey this picture. Let us assume that we are actually taking a physical picture of the power of thought, using the mind as the sensitive plate of the camera and controlled habit as the lens, through which any desired object may be photographed.

The plate of the camera will register any object reflected upon it through the lens. It does not pick and choose, but registers everything that is cast upon it, whether good or bad. To make a clear picture, the lens must be properly focussed and the object to be photographed must be flooded with the proper amount of light, all of which depends upon the skill of the person operating the camera.

Thus, the operator works through controlled habit! He does not register the picture on the plate of the camera; the light and the chemicals on the surface of the 'sensitised' plate do the registering; but the operator does choose the object to be photographed. He times the exposure so as to give it the proper amount of light, and he focusses the lens so it will pick up the proper details of the object to be photographed. The picture he gets will be in exact proportion to his skill in controlling all these factors. He may also choose the object which he photographs.

Now let me shift the scene from the camera to the human brain and see how perfectly the two resemble one another in the manner of their operation. The individual chooses the subject he wishes to register in the cells of his brain, the brain serving as the plate of the camera. He calls the subject chosen a Definite Major Purpose. He wants the brain to pick up a clear picture of the object of that purpose, register it, and turn it over to his subconscious mind for translation into its physical reality. Therefore, he proceeds, through the principle of controlled habit, to place in his conscious mind a picture of that which he wants. Day by day, he recreates that picture (through controlled habit), recognising, as the skilled thinker does, that the mental impulse of thought through which he is painting the picture in his brain must be given the right amount of time (through repeated exposures) to register, and it must also be accompanied by the proper proportion of 'light' (emotional feeling) to enable the brain to pick up a clear outline of the thought.

In this process of painting in the brain, a clear picture of a purpose one desires to achieve, one either consciously or unconsciously uses the 'mechanism' of the brain, as described in Chart Number 2. Therefore, let us turn back to that chart and retrace the steps one must take.

First step: The adoption of a Definite Major Purpose.

Second step: The creation of a practical plan for attaining the purpose.

Third step: A Master Mind alliance with others whose experience, education, skill and influence may be needed.

Fourth step: Immediate action in carrying out the plan adopted.

Observe that all four steps are well within the possibility of easy control of anyone, but nothing will happen unless all four steps are taken and persistently carried out to their logical conclusion. This calls for controlled habit! It calls for constant application of the necessary habits until the object desired has been attained.

Here, then, enters the effect of controlled habit upon social heredity. After one voluntarily proceeds to carry out one's plans, in the attainment of one's Definite Major Purpose, the law of social heredity fixes one's actions in the form of permanent habits; both physical habits and habits of thought; however, soon after controlled habit is used, the subconscious section of the mind takes over the controlled habit and carries it out to its logical conclusion by whatever practical means available.

This does not mean, however, that the job should be left entirely to the subconscious mind. The individual must proceed on his own account, just as if he expected no help from his subconscious mind. What the subconscious mind actually does is this: It inspires one (through the faculty of imagination) with ideas, plans, and ways and means of attaining the object of his purpose, and that is all that need be expected of it.

In taking the four steps here described, one must make use of all the principles of this philosophy outlined in Chart Number 2, all of which constitute a part of that which we call controlled habit. These principles will not work merely by one's having read and understood them. They must be put into action! The action must be persisted in until it becomes fixed habit. I am repeating this in many different ways because to overlook it will mean defeat. Thus, your own controlled habit may supplant the habits which environment had originally suggested.

Organised thinking consists of persistent action in applying any combination of the principles of this philosophy. Without action, there will be no controlled habits. Without controlled habits, there will be no dependable registration in the brain of the picture of that which one desires. Therefore, there will be nothing which the subconscious mind can take over and act upon.

Now let us turn to Chart Number 3 and study the sources of power and the faculties of the mind which are involved in taking the four steps I have described.

The source of all power of thought is Infinite Intelligence, shown at the top of the chart. This intelligence cannot be directly appropriated by the brain of man (for reasons with which no one is familiar). Therefore, the Creator has provided man with a connecting link between Infinite Intelligence and the brain, known as the subconscious section of the mind. The subconscious mind serves as a 'mixing chamber' in which the desires of man are given the creative power necessary to enable him to convert them into any forms of physical equivalents he chooses.

Next on the chart is the faculty of willpower. This is under one's control, and it is the major tool with which controlled habits are formed. (If one does not form one's own habits, by the power of one's will, 'tramp' habits will take possession of the mind, corresponding, precisely, to the nature of one's environmental influences. These stray habits are formed through the law of social heredity.)

The faculty of the will is the 'boss' of all other departments of the mind. It can make habits and it can unmake them. It can choose aims and purposes, and it can change them. It can countermand any desire of the emotions, and set aside any decision of the faculty of reason. It can even set aside any decision of the conscience.

The faculty of the will is the tool with which one paints a clear picture of that which one desires, and it does this by presenting that picture in the conscious mind repeatedly. This repetition of desire or purpose, followed by appropriate action in carrying out the desire or purpose, is the method by which controlled habit is formed.

If the faculty of the will is sufficiently determined (as it is when one's Definite Major Purpose is an obsession), it can and it does call into action every other region of the mind. It commands the emotions to go into action and they comply. It heeds the faculty of reason, or refuses to do so. It directs the faculty of the imagination to work out ways and means of attaining desired ends, and that faculty goes to work. It digs deeply into the storehouse of the memory and brings out such materials (knowledge, experience, etc.) as are available there. It spurs the subconscious section of the mind into action and causes it to call in a greater flow of Infinite Intelligence.

It simulates the 'sixth sense' and puts the principle of intuition into operation. But, remember always that it does these things only when backed and inspired by a strong desire, or an obsessional motive, in the form of a Definite Purpose.

The starting point of controlled habit, therefore, is definiteness of purpose. If that purpose is obsessional, in proportion, it is picked up immediately by the faculty of the will. If the purpose is vague, or lacking in emotional desire, the faculty of the will have no part of it, and nothing will happen.

It might be said, therefore, that the emotions serve as a medium for building a fire under the faculty of the will, to start it into action. Organised thought is a mixture of the power of will and the power of the emotions, properly balanced and directed to the attainment of definite ends. Disorganised thought is that which is inspired by the emotions, without the modifying influence of the will – that is, emotion without control. That sort of thought is without value. It may be, and it usually is, very dangerous. It always is dangerous if it is not modified by the faculty of reason. The faculty of willpower is the medium that may be used to balance the relationship between the emotions and the faculty of reason.

How Habits are Formed

Habits are formed in two ways. One is by voluntary repetition of any desired thought or action, using the willpower, if necessary, to enforce the repetition. Most voluntary habits, however, grow out of the repeated expression of a desire based on definite motive. Motive is the greatest of all the media for the formation of habits.

The other type of habit is involuntary. It develops, through the law of social heredity, from one's environmental influences. Such habits are not controlled. Such habits follow the line of least resistance. They lead to procrastination, indifference, and indefiniteness, ending finally in forcing the individual into what is commonly called a 'rut'. Let it be remembered that the law of social heredity is always and everywhere in operation; that it directs men's thoughts and action habits.

After any habit has been well established by repetition of thought or physical action, it automatically expresses itself through physical activity appropriate to its nature. Attention should be given to controlling the habits of thought since all thought habits reflect themselves, in one way or another, through physical action. All physical action, therefore, begins in the form of a thought. To control physical action, one has only to control thoughts. The presence of any thought in the mind has a tendency to set up an appropriate physical action in some portion of the body.

I have emphasised the importance of voluntary, controlled action of both the physical body and the mind. While it is true that the mere presence of any thought in the mind has a tendency to set up an appropriate physical action in the body, it is a tendency only. Successful people cannot wait on 'tendencies'. They must adopt and apply dependable rules that bring desired results, and bring them when and where they are needed. Therefore, any habit one wishes to develop should be voluntarily begun and repeated indefinitely, until it becomes automatic in its functioning. There is no other way of developing desirable habits. Habits of any other nature are not controlled, but, on the other hand, they control the individual, leading him to misery, poverty and failure more often than to success.

The method by which habits are formed may be compared with the method by which a 'rut' is cut in a dirt road by the wheels of a wagon. One time over, the road makes a slight indenture in the dirt. A second trip makes a deeper indenture, and so on, until finally the 'rut' becomes so deep that when once the wheels fall into it, they are guided by it. Finally, if unattended, the 'rut' becomes a small gulley so great as to impede progress entirely.

The mind works in precisely the same manner. One thought of a given subject makes only a slight impression on the brain. A repetition of that thought makes a deeper impression, and many repetitions make the impression so deep that it, too, becomes a 'mental rut' into which the 'wheels' of thought fall and operate automatically. If the gulley is not stopped, it will in time become so serious that it will demoralise thought.

Émile Coué had this principle of thought habit in mind when he admonished his followers to repeat, many times daily, his famous health and success formula, 'Day by day, in every way, I am becoming better and better.' To the person unfamiliar with the manner in which thought habits are formed, such a formula might seem useless; but not so with the person who understands how the power of thought operates.

You will know when a habit has been properly established by your own state of mind and by the results you get from it. When the habit has been properly developed you will experience a feeling of continuous enthusiasm in connection with your plans. This enthusiasm will drive you during your every conscious moment. It will even continue driving you, through your subconscious mind, while you sleep, and you need not be surprised when your subconscious mind awakens you from sleep, with some idea or plan useful in carrying out the object of your Definite Major Purpose. Work will no longer be a drudge. It will be a pleasure in which you will engage as eagerly as you eat your meals when hungry. Moreover, things will begin to happen outside your own mind that will give you courage. People will begin to cooperate with you in a spirit of enthusiasm. Unexpected opportunities for the promotion of your personal interests and plans will spring up all around you. Your imagination will become keener and more active. You can work long hours without becoming fatigued. You will experience better health than you ever had before. Gradually, the dark glasses of despair you have been wearing will change their colour and you will see the whole world around you through crystal-clear glasses of hope and faith, for you will have changed the entire vibration of your being, and with this change will come an improvement in your financial, social, and occupational status.

This is no idle promise! I know it will be realised by you, if you follow instructions, because it has happened to thousands of other students of this philosophy. Defeat may overtake you, as it overtakes everyone; but you will use it as a challenge to greater effort, because you will have discovered that organised thought is an irresistible force capable of making stepping-stones out of stumbling blocks.

How, may I ask, could anyone be permanently defeated who has acquired the ability to transmute every emotion, every feeling, every fear, and every worry into a constructive positive driving force for the attainment of definite ends? And this is precisely what organised thought enables one to do.

> EVERY student of this philosophy should have the word ACTION burned into his consciousness, for it is one of the keywords of the entire philosophy.
>
> —Andrew Carnegie

□

Andrew Carnegie's Views on Organised Thinking

This interview took place in Mr. Carnegie's private study, more than thirty years ago, while the great steel master was coaching his protégé, Napoleon Hill, in preparation for the organisation of the Philosophy of American Achievement.

HILL:

You have explained that an important principle of individual achievement is Organised Thought. You have stated, also, that no one may be sure of success without the ability to organise his thinking habits. Therefore, will you go ahead, Mr. Carnegie, and explain the meaning of the term 'organised thought'? I have a general idea what it means, but I would like to have a detailed statement of its meaning – also a clear understanding of how this principle is applied in the practical affairs of life.

CARNEGIE:

Before discussing the organisation of thought, let us examine thought itself. What is thought? With what do we think? Is thought subject to individual control?

Thought is a form of energy that is distributed through the brain, but it has one peculiar quality unknown in connection with all other forms of energy; it has intelligence!

Thought can be controlled and directed towards the attainment of anything man may desire. In fact, thought is the only thing over which any person has complete, unchallenged control. The system of control is so complete that no one may penetrate the mind of another without his consent, although this system of protection often is so loosely guarded that one's mind may be entered at will by any person skilled in the art of thought interpretation. Many people not only leave their minds wide open for others to enter and interpret their thoughts, but they voluntarily disclose the nature of their thoughts by unguarded expressions of speech and their personal conduct, their facial expression, and the like.

HILL:

Is it safe for one to leave his mind open to free entry by others?

CARNEGIE:

Just about as safe as leaving the door to one's house unlocked, with all of one's valuables left inside the house, except that the loss of purely material things is as nothing compared with the loss one may suffer by leaving his mind open to entry by any stray tramp who may wish to go in and take possession.

You see, the habit of leaving one's mind open and unguarded not only permits other people to enter and become familiar with one's most private thoughts, but this habit permits all sorts of 'tramp' thoughts, released from the minds of others, to enter one's mind.

HILL:

You believe, then, that thoughts do pass from one mind to another.

CARNEGIE:

Yes, one's mind is being constantly bombarded with the impulses of thought released from the minds of others – especially those with whom we come into close contact daily. One negative-minded workman, if left to associate with other workmen, will pass on his negative thoughts to every other person within the range of his influence, although he never speaks a word or makes a single move indicating his state of mind. I have seen this very thing happen so often that I could not be mistaken about it.

HILL:

And that is why you emphasise, so strongly, the necessity of harmony between men associated in a Master Mind alliance?

CARNEGIE:

That is one of the major reasons why I have emphasised

the importance of harmony. The 'chemistry' of the brain is such that the mind power of a group of men can be organised so it functions as one unit of power only when there is perfect rapport between the minds of the individuals.

HILL:

One of the important steps, in organised thought, seems to be that of the Master Mind alliance, through which men pool their mind power, their experience, education, and knowledge, and move in response to a common motive. Is this the right idea, Mr. Carnegie?

CARNEGIE:

You have stated the matter perfectly. You might have said that the Master Mind alliance is the most important step one may take in connection with organised thought, for that is true. But organised thought begins with the organisation of the individual's thinking habits. To become an effective member of a Master Mind alliance, an individual must first form definite, controlled habits of thought! A group of men working together under the Master Mind principle, each of whom has so disciplined himself that he controls his thought habits, represents organised thought of the highest order. As a matter of fact, there never can be full assurance of harmony in a Master Mind group unless each member of the group is so self-disciplined that he can control his own thoughts.

HILL:

Do I understand you to say that an individual may actually discipline himself so that he controls the nature of his thoughts?

CARNEGIE:

Yes, that is true, but remember that one gains control over his thoughts by forming definite thought habits. You know, of course, that when habits are once formed, they function automatically, without any voluntary effort on the individual's part.

HILL:

But Mr. Carnegie, isn't it very difficult for one to force his mind to function through definite habits? How may one go about this sort of self-discipline?

CARNEGIE:

No, there is nothing difficult about the formation of habits. As a matter of fact, the mind is constantly forming thought habits without the conscious knowledge of the individual, responding, as the mind does, to every influence that reaches it from one's daily environment. Through self-discipline, one may switch the action of his mind from responses to the casual influences around him to subjects of his own choice instead. This is accomplished by setting up in the mind a definite motive, based on a definite purpose, and intensifying that purpose until it becomes an obsession.

Stating the matter differently, one may fill his mind with a definite purpose that is so interesting, it leaves him no time or opportunity to dwell upon other subjects. In this manner, he forms definite thought habits. The mind responds to whatever stimuli one feeds it. When a man is driven by a strong desire to achieve success in any given direction, his mind responds to that desire and forms definite thought habits connected with the attainment of that desire.

HILL:

Then organised thought begins with definiteness of purpose?

CARNEGIE:

Everything man achieves begins with definiteness of purpose. Name a single instance, if you can, where a man has achieved any form of success without a definite motive, based on a definite purpose, carried out through a definite plan.

But, you must remember that there is one more factor that must be considered in connection with definiteness of purpose. The purpose must be expressed in terms of intense action. Here is where the power of the emotions gives an account of itself. The emotional feeling of desire for the attainment of a definite purpose is the power that gives life and action to that purpose, and influences one to move on his own initiative. To ensure satisfactory results, one's definite purpose should be given obsessional proportions. It should be backed by a burning desire for its attainment. Desires of this sort take full possession of one's mind and keep it so fully occupied that it has no inclination or opportunity to entertain stray thoughts released by the minds of others.

HILL:

I believe I see what you mean. For example, a young man who is in love has no difficulty in keeping his mind on the object of his love, and not infrequently does his mind work out ways and means of inducing a response to his affections, from the woman of his choice. In this sort of circumstance, one has no difficulty in forming controlled thought habits.

CARNEGIE:

Your illustration is perfect! Now switch it over to some other sort of purpose such, for example, as the development of a business, or a profession, or the attainment of a definite position, or the accumulation of money, and you will have an idea of how these ends are attained, through obsessional desire for their attainment.

HILL:

But, Mr. Carnegie, one usually cannot put the same sort of emotional desire into the attainment of material things that he experiences in his love for the woman of his choice.

CARNEGIE:

No, of course not; but there are other emotions with which he can stimulate his desire for material things. Study the nine basic motives and you will observe that any sort of a desire is emotional in its nature. There is the desire for material riches, and it is a rather universal and well developed desire with most people; the desire for personal expression leading to recognition and fame; the desire for self preservation; and the desire for freedom of body and mind. All of one's emotions, including, of course, the emotion of love, can be converted to the attainment of any desired end. The desire for the accumulation of material riches may, for example, be combined with one's love for the woman of his choice, where the desire for money is associated with one's desire to provide the woman of his choice with the comforts that money will buy. In such a circumstance, one would have a double motive for the accumulation of money.

HILL:

Oh, yes! I see what you mean. As a matter of fact, one might be influenced by all of the seven positive motives, as a driving force behind one's major purpose in life, could he not?

CARNEGIE

Yes, by the seven positive motives and, through transmutation of emotion, by the two negative motives as well. You know, of course, that any emotion, whether positive or negative, may become an inspiration to action that can be directed to the attainment of any desired end. The motive of fear, for example, often serves as a powerful inspiration to action. To benefit by it, one has only to control his action habits, until those habits become automatic.

HILL:

Do you mean that habits function voluntarily, without any effort on the part of an individual?

CARNEGIE:

Yes, that is exactly what any habit does when it becomes fixed.

HILL:

You say 'when it becomes fixed'? What fixes a habit? Must an individual do that, and if so, how does he proceed to make a habit permanent?

CARNEGIE:

Habits become fixed by some unknown law of nature which causes the impulses of thought to be taken over by the subconscious mind and voluntarily carried out. This law does not make habits. It only fixes them so they operate automatically. The individual begins a habit by repeating a thought or a physical act. After a time (depending upon the emotional feeling that goes into the thought) one's thought habits are taken over and followed voluntarily.

HILL:

Then the formation of habits is something an individual may control?

CARNEGIE:

Oh, yes! And may I remind you that the control of habit forming is an important part of organised thinking? You see, an individual may set up any sort of habits he chooses, go through them for a while, very much in the same manner that one would go through with a physical culture sitting up exercise, after which the habits will become automatically perpetuated without his conscious attention to them.

HILL:

And you say that some unknown law of nature fixes one's habits, so they perpetuate themselves?

CARNEGIE:

Yes, that is an established fact. It is one of the most important facts in the entire field of mental phenomena, for it is literally the medium by which an individual may take possession of his own mind! The man who uncovers the secret by which nature fixes man's habits will have made a stupendous contribution to science – a greater contribution, perhaps, than that made by Newton, who discovered the law of gravitation. Perhaps when the discovery is made, if it ever is made, it will be revealed that the law which fixes men's habits and the law of gravitation are closely related, if not actually one and the same.

HILL:

Your hypothesis intrigues me, Mr. Carnegie! Could you elaborate upon it?

All we know definitely about habit is the fact that any thought or physical act that is repeated tends to become perpetuated, through some force which carries on the habit automatically. We know that habits can be changed, modified, or eliminated altogether, by the simple process of voluntarily adopting opposing habits of a stronger nature. For example, the habit of procrastination (a habit with which everyone is more or less afflicted) can be mastered by setting up definite habits of prompt initiative, based on a sufficiently strong motive to ensure the new habits a dominating influence in the mind until they become automatic in their operation.

Thus, you see that motive and habit are twin brothers! Almost every habit one adopts voluntarily is the result of a definite motive, or purpose. You see, therefore, that one may establish any habit he desires, or eliminate any undesirable habit, by applying enough self-discipline to fix his habits until they become automatic. If habits are not fixed voluntarily, they develop without one's conscious help. It is in this manner that most undesirable habits are formed.

HILL:

It is obvious, then, that the principle of self-discipline is a necessary tool in the formation of habits one deliberately forms?

CARNEGIE:

Yes, self-discipline and organised thinking are almost synonymous terms. There can be no organised thinking without strict self-discipline, for after all, organised thought is nothing but carefully chosen thought. Thought habits can be established only through strict self-discipline. Motive, or obsessional desire, makes self-discipline very easy. It is no trouble at all to form thought habits if one has a definite motive, backed by a strong emotional desire for the attainment of the object of the motive.

HILL:

Do you mean that it is easy for one to form thought habits in connection with subjects in which one has a keen personal interest?

CARNEGIE:

That's the idea, exactly. The procrastinator drifts through life, a failure, because he has no obsessional motive for doing anything in particular. His thinking is not organised because he has chosen no specific calling for organised planning.

HILL:

Mr. Carnegie, will you briefly describe the major benefits of organised thinking, from the viewpoint of the man who wishes to make the best use of his time and ability?

CARNEGIE:

The benefits are so numerous that it is difficult to decide where to begin or where to stop, but these are some of the more obvious advantages of this habit:

(a) Organised thinking enables one to become the master of his own mind. This he accomplishes by training his faculty of will to control his emotions, turning them on and off as occasion may require.

(b) Organised thinking forces one to work with definiteness of purpose, thereby enabling him to set up a habit that prohibits procrastination.
(c) It develops the habit of working with definite plans instead of blundering ahead by the hit-or-miss method.
(d) It enables one to stimulate the subconscious mind to greater action and more ready response, in the attainment of desired ends, instead of allowing the subconscious mind to respond to the 'tramp' thoughts and destructive influences of one's environment.
(e) It develops self-reliance.
(f) It gives one the benefit of the knowledge, experience, and education of others, through the medium of the Master Mind alliance, which is an important medium used by all able thinkers.
(g) It enables one to convert his efforts into greater material resources and larger income, since an organised mind can produce more than one that is not organised.
(h) It develops the habit of accurate analysis, through which one may find the solution to his problems instead of worrying over them.
(i) It aids in maintaining sound health, because mind power that is organised and directed towards the attainment of desirable ends has no time to be wasted in connection with self-pity or imaginary ailments. Idle minds tend to develop ailing bodies.
(j) Last, but by no means least, organised thinking leads to peace of mind and that form of permanent happiness which is known only to the man who keeps his mind fully occupied. No one can be either happy or successful without a planned program for the use of his time. Planned programs are based on organised thinking.

As I have stated before, the brain is something like a rich garden spot in that it will voluntarily grow a fine crop of weeds if it is not organised and kept busy growing a more desirable crop. The weeds are represented by the stray thoughts that take possession of the unorganised, idle mind, as the result of one's daily environment.

Study this list of benefits carefully and you will reach the conclusion that any one of them offers sufficient reward to justify all the effort one puts into organising his thinking habits. The sum total of all these benefits represents the difference between success and failure. Success is always the result of an ordered life. An ordered life comes through organised thinking and carefully controlled habits.

HILL:

I take it, from what you have said, that work and organised thinking are essentially related.

CARNEGIE:

Nothing can take the place of work, as a part of organised thinking. You see, work is thought power translated into physical action! Organised thinking can never be relied upon to become a habit until it is expressed in some form of action.

HILL:

You have stated that organised thinking begins with the adoption of a Definite Purpose; that the purpose must be followed by a plan, expressed in action until the action becomes a habit. Now, will you state whether or not one may work as effectively in expressing a plan of action in connection with some form of labour he does not like to perform as he can if he performs work that he likes?

CARNEGIE:

A man will always be more effective when engaged in the sort of work he likes best. That is why, one's major purpose in life should be of his own choice. People who drift through life, performing work they do not like, merely because they must have an income as a means of living, seldom get more than a living from their labour. You see, this sort of labour does not inspire one to perform service in an obsessional desire to work. It is one of the tragedies of civilisation that we have not found a way to give every man the sort of work he likes best to do. That sort of work is never a drudgery.

HILL:

Then it would be proper to say that organised thinking can best be done when a man moves with a definite motive, in the performance of work of his own choice, under conditions that inspire him to make his work an obsessional desire?

CARNEGIE:

That would be one way of stating the matter. You will observe, as you begin to analyse men who succeed and those who fail, that the successful men always are engaged in work they like to perform. Hours mean nothing to them. They consider the joy of their labour to be an important part – perhaps the most important part – of their compensation.

HILL:

Do you think the time will ever come when ordered society will find ways and means of aiding everyone to do that which he likes best to do?

CARNEGIE:

Yes, I think that time will come, because that sort of a system would be not only economical, but it would do away with much of the misunderstanding that now prevails between employers and employees. The man who is engaged in work of his own choice is worth much more than the man who performs work that he does not like, no matter what the wage scale may be.

HILL:

Isn't it the responsibility of the employers to find a way to assign all workmen to the sort of work they like best?

CARNEGIE:

Perhaps it is, but our present system of industry does not always make this an easy matter You see, there are only a certain number of jobs of each class of work to be performed in a business or industry, and generally the ones men like best to do are those of which there are the fewest number. The solution of this problem will call for an improved system of employment – one that will enable an employer to select men who are suited for each particular job, with reference to their native ability, training, and preference for jobs. It will also call for a different system of compensation – a system that will give men an opportunity to earn more money when performing work that is less desirable, thereby establishing a motive for their putting more into such work.

HILL:

I can see that the analysis of this subject leads one, immediately, into deep water. It seems that the solution of the problem will have to begin while the individual is being educated, through a system that will prepare him to perform work of his own choice. Then, all educational institutions should coordinate their efforts in such a manner that they would not turn out too many men for some types of work and too few for other types. This would require a periodic survey of industry, business, and the professions, to enable educational institutions to determine how many men of each classification could be absorbed in employment.

CARNEGIE:

Yes, the system would have to be conducted in some such manner. Right now, for example, the schools are turning out doctors, teachers, and lawyers in greater numbers than are needed in these fields, with the result that some of the members of these professions have a hard time making a living.

HILL:

I take it, from your analysis, that organised thinking should begin with those engaged in educational work and those who manage industry and business.

CARNEGIE:

Yes, that is one place where it should begin, but do not overlook the fact that the habit of organised thinking is also an individual responsibility, and the individual who overlooks it must accept from life whatever he can get. The better things of life go always to men who form habits of organised thinking. It has always been this way. It always will be. Thinking constructively is one responsibility which no one can delegate to another. It is an individual responsibility.

HILL:

Granted, Mr. Carnegie, that organised thinking is an individual responsibility, there must be a starting point from which one begins to acquire the ability to organise his thinking, and at least a few simple rules by which one may be guided in this business of organising his thoughts. Could you name some of the rules?

CARNEGIE:

Well, the first thing one must recognise, in order to become an accurate thinker, is the known fact that the power with which we think is 'mental dynamite' that can be organised and used constructively for the attainment of definite ends, but if it is not organised and used, through controlled habits, it may become a 'mental explosive' that will literally blast one's hopes of achievement and lead to inevitable failure.

Stating the matter in another way, one should recognise that the power of thought is probably a projected portion of Infinite Intelligence, but every individual has been given the privilege of appropriating and using this power for the attainment of ends of his own choice; that the medium of appropriation and control is voluntary habits! One cannot control Infinite Intelligence, but one can control his own mental and physical habits, thus indirectly he may appropriate and use Infinite Intelligence, because Infinite Intelligence fixes one's habits and makes them permanent and automatic in their operation.

Next, the accurate thinker must learn how to avail himself of reliable sources of information; where to obtain dependable facts which he will need in connection with organised thinking. Guesswork and hopeful wishing (the most common sources of information to a majority of the people) can never be relied upon to supplant accurate sources of facts.

Here is where the Master Mind principle becomes indispensable, as it enables one to supplement his own stock of knowledge with the knowledge, education, experience, and native ability of all others with whom he has a Master Mind alliance. If one chooses his Master Mind allies wisely, as most successful business and industrial leaders choose theirs, one may have at his command the most reliable sources of knowledge that schooling and human experience have to offer. Thus, in his business of thinking, planning, and organising, he has not merely his own brain to guide him, but the brains of each member of his Master Mind alliance.

There is no escape from the fact that the formation of a Master Mind alliance is one of the most important major steps one must take in order to organise his thinking, evidence of which may be found in the fact that all successful people are allied, in one way or another, with others whose knowledge they use freely. Without such an alliance, there can be no such reality as effectively organised thinking, and this for the reason that one brain (no matter how capable it may be) is never complete by itself. When we speak of a man's wife as his 'better half' we generally express much more of the truth than we realise, for it is a well-known fact that no man's mind is complete without a harmonious alliance with the mind of a woman. Therefore, every man should include at least one woman in his Master Mind alliance. When the minds of male and female are combined, or blended, in a spirit of harmony, the alliance tunes in and appropriates a much greater proportion of that force which we call 'spiritual power' than either can appropriate when operating independently. The man who overlooks this truth will suffer an irreparable loss of potential mind power, as there is nothing that can take the place of spiritual power.

Now, I cannot tell you what spiritual power' really is, but I assume that it is simply a greater volume of Infinite Intelligence than that which is available where the feeling we describe as 'spiritual' is not present. There are certain emotions which lift one into this exalted feeling, such as the emotion of love and the emotion of faith. While one's mind is stimulated by this exalted feeling, the faculty of the imagination becomes more alert, one's words take on a magnetic influence that makes them impressive, fear and self-limitation disappear, and one dares to undertake tasks he would not think of beginning when his mind is stimulated only by the purely mental processes of enthusiasm and desire.

HILL:

Do you mean, Mr. Carnegie, that one may so relate himself to others under the Master Mind principle, that he may lift himself above the ordinary processes of mental operation of the mind, and place himself under the guiding influence of that power known as spiritual? And this, too, is a part of organised thinking?

CARNEGIE:

I mean precisely that! The term 'organised thinking' means everything the two words connote. That is, thinking based on every known advantage, every known mind stimulant, every known source of accurate knowledge, and the highest form of ability, whether it be native ability or acquired ability; whether it be individual ability or the ability available to one through the minds of others.

HILL:

Pardon my seeming facetiousness, but I take it from what you have just said that a man who is highly skilled as an organised thinker is a sort of super-man!

CARNEGIE:

To be candid, you are correct! And I am glad to know that you have at last caught the full significance of what I have been trying to tell you; namely, that the power of thought is an irresistible force; that it has no limitations save those set up by the individual, either by his lack of understanding of the possibilities of thought power, or lack of knowledge as to how to organise, appropriate and supply this power.

HILL:

What about the man who acquires great knowledge in connection with organised thinking, but uses his power unfairly, to gain advantage over others? Is there not a danger in teaching men how to become supermen, in view of the fact that some men have great capacity to use their minds, but lack a well-grounded sense of moral obligation to others?

CARNEGIE:

An all-wise Creator has provided for such a circumstance, evidence of which may be found in the fact that the man who uses his mind power to damage or destroy others soon eliminates himself by the loss of his power, and the Creator has also very wisely provided that this sort of power is something that cannot be passed on from one to another, through physical heredity. It is a power that each individual must acquire for himself, or he does not become privileged to benefit by it.

Go back into history and examine the records of those who have undertaken to become world conquerors, and observe what happened to them! Nero, Alexander the Great, Julius Caesar, Napoleon Bonaparte, and others of similar determination made great strides towards world domination; but look what happened to them and their achievements. Not one of them accomplished his aim, not one of them passed on to his followers any means by which his gains could be maintained; but these selfish leaders did pass on to their followers a curse that wiped out all the gains they made.

Apply the principle anywhere you choose, at any period of civilisation, and observe that the effect is the same. Only the gains of men who used their mind power beneficially have been preserved. Study the gains made by the Nazarene, for example, and observe that although they were infinitesimal during his lifetime, they have lived and spread down through nineteen centuries until the influence of Christianity is now a recognised force in every part of the world.

Give yourself no worry over the man who uses his mind power for the detriment of others, for he has fixed his own destiny by the nature of his deeds. If he is not cut down sooner, he will be wiped out within the accepted three score and ten years of average age that men live. The trend of civilisation is upward, and though the line may zigzag upward and downward at given periods, it moves eternally upward, as a whole. Wise men recognise this truth and adapt themselves to it.

HILL:

I agree with what you have said, Mr. Carnegie, but there are so few wise men! The world seems populated with too many who either fail to recognise the advantages of relating themselves to others helpfully, or grossly neglect to do so, believing, no doubt, that they are smart enough to make their own rules of life and get by with them. What should be done with, or for, such people? Should they not be either taught, or forcefully made to conform to the rules of decent human relationship?

CARNEGIE:

Yes, they are forced to conform, to a certain extent. Practically, every man-made law that exists is evidence of the recognition of the need of a means of restraint. If everyone understood and respected the laws of nature, there would be no need for man-made laws. But force is not enough to bring men into an understanding of the laws of nature. Education is also necessary. That is why you were chosen to organise the Philosophy of American Achievement. In this philosophy, you have the necessary motives and inducements, in the form of promise of individual benefits, to influence people to apply the philosophy voluntarily and of their own free will. This sort of effort is far superior to that which is produced through force. Men do best that which they wish to do!

HILL:

Oh, I see what you mean! It is better to teach a person to adapt himself to rules of human relationship that are beneficial to others as well as himself than it is to force him to do so. Is that your idea?

CARNEGIE:

That is the idea, exactly! In rearing children, for example, it is far better to induce a child to wish to do something than it is to use force. Parents who understand this psychology manage their children by directing their interests to things that are helpful to them and not objectionable to others, rather than by forcing them to refrain from doing objectionable things.

In a sense, we adults are only little children, and we do best that which we have been influenced to wish to do. We also resent being forced to do or to refrain from doing anything! This is an inherent part of human nature. It is a part of everyone, at all ages.

Everyone likes freedom to act on his own initiative. Destroy this freedom and you retard the mental and spiritual growth of the individual. You might say, also, that you destroy economic and financial achievements the moment you destroy the desire for personal initiative.

It is a recognised fact that the people of the United States enjoy the highest standard of living known in the history of the world. With this known fact, consider, also, the fact that the American people are distinguished because of their natural inclination to become self-determining, and the further fact that we have more personal freedom than any other people have had. The whole system of free enterprise, under the American way of life, is the nearest approach to adaptation to nature's plan for the growth of man through self-effort that the world has ever known.

HILL:

Then organised thinking and the privilege of free, unmodified, personal initiative are closely related, are they not?

CARNEGIE:

You have the right idea. Organised Thought must be followed by expression, through organised plans of action! One does not grow mentally or spiritually by passive thought alone. Growth is the result of thought expressed through voluntarily developed and definitely controlled habits of action.

HILL:

And, that is why, the man with practical experience in the application of any form of theoretical knowledge has more ability than the man who has only the theory, is it not, Mr. Carnegie?

CARNEGIE:

You have hit the nail squarely on the head. Ability, in its most effective form, is based upon sound theory expressed in definitely organised forms of action. That is why most college graduates have to acquire practical experience in the application of the knowledge gained from their schooling, before they become efficient.

HILL:

Would you say, then, that organised thinking is a combination of knowledge and organised action in the expression of knowledge?

CARNEGIE:

I would say precisely that! Knowledge has no value what soever unless and until it is expressed in terms of organised action. This explains why the man with nothing but 'book learning' is seldom practical in the application of knowledge gained from books alone.

HILL:

But, book learning is helpful, is it not?

CARNEGIE:

Yes, book learning is essential as a foundation of education, but remember that it is only a foundation. An educated person is one who has so developed his mind, through a combination of knowledge and the expression of knowledge, that he can reshape any set of circumstances to meet the requirements of his desires. That sort of ability consists of both theory and practice, mostly the latter.

A man might read every book ever written on engineering; yet he would be unable to lay out a plan and build a bridge until he had combined his theoretical knowledge with practical experience. Of course, he could build a bridge on theory alone, but there would be no assurance that it would stand under any given weight. Practical engineers know precisely how much weight a bridge will carry, and they know how to supervise the building of such a bridge so it can be depended upon.

HILL:

Could a man become an able salesman by reading, alone?

CARNEGIE:

The principle of combining theory with practice applies the same to salesmanship as to salesmanship as to the building of bridges, or anything else.

The principle is fundamental. Therefore, it is an essential part of organised thinking. A man does not become an able lawyer, or dentist, or doctor by merely acquiring a degree in these professions. He becomes able by applying the theory he learns in school, in the practical field of experience, and in no other way. There is no school that equals the good old University of Experience, and this is one school in which 'cribbing' is not possible. One either graduates on merit or one does not graduate at all. Cheating is impossible! And the teacher is the individual himself. When a man enters the University of Experience, he stands, at last, in front of one counter on which the merchandise is plainly marked and he is both the salesman and the purchaser. If he gets the merchandise he desires, he pays the price that life has placed upon it.

HILL:

From all you have said on the subject of organised thinking, Mr. Carnegie, I reach the conclusion that skill is developed in this art first, by coordination between the faculties of the mind and the physical body, through definitely controlled habits; and second, by coordination with one's associates, under the Master Mind principle, for the attainment of definite objectives.

CARNEGIE:

You have come pretty near to describing the modus operandi of organised thinking, but you should have emphasised one thing you omitted, the necessity of action! You are correct in stating that organised thinking begins by coordination between the faculties of the mind and the physical means of expressing thought, but do not forget that skill and perfection are attained only by highly developed and definitely controlled habits of action! I have repeated this idea, over and over again – not that I do not believe you understand it, but for the reason that I know, from association with thousands of men, how long it requires to get one to become aware of the importance of this point.

Unless a man becomes 'action-conscious', he will never become an organised thinker. He may think from morning until night, but unless he puts his thoughts into action he will be nothing but a daydreamer. He may theorise, but he will never learn to build a bridge, or perform any sort of practical service. Right here is where many people deceive themselves into believing that they are thinkers. I have heard not a few men say, "I have been thinking of doing this or that, but so far I have found no way to do it." Now, what is the trouble with such men? They have left out of their thinking one important factor, and that is physical action!

If you wish to do something, start right where you stand, and begin doing it – NOW!

'What,' you may ask, "shall I use for tools? Where will I get the capital? Who will help me?"

And I shall reply that men who accomplish anything worthy of mention always begin before everything they need is in hand. I have never yet been entirely ready for anything I have begun, and I doubt if anyone else ever has been. It is one of the strange phenomena of human experience that the man who begins, where he stands, and does the best he can with whatever means he may have, very soon finds other and better means of accomplishing his objectives. Mysteriously, the tools are placed at his disposal.

This question of one's not being ready usually is nothing but an excuse with which he deceives himself. You were not ready to begin organising the world's first practical philosophy of individual achievement. You needed more schooling. You needed a monetary subsidy to carry you through twenty years of profitless research. You needed age and maturity of thought, and you needed practical experience in many different fields of endeavour. Yes, you needed all these things, and many more, before presenting the world with a dependable philosophy of achievement. But, what did you do when I gave you your opportunity to organise such a philosophy? I'll tell you what you did. Within twenty-nine seconds of the time that I gave you the opportunity, you grabbed it and went to work on it and I would stake my life that nothing but death could stop you from finishing the job. Men who start where they stand, when they wish to do something, usually find a way of finishing that which they undertake.

I keep a watch in my desk for the sole purpose of timing men's reactions to ideas and opportunities. That watch has ticked off the destiny of hundreds of men to whom I have given opportunities for self-advancement. The watch never lies! It tells exactly how long it takes a man to make up his mind when he has all the necessary information before him to enable him to reach a decision. It tells precisely how much action consciousness a man has. Your reaction time was twenty-nine seconds. You had thirty-one seconds still to go when you reached a decision and embraced the opportunity I gave you. If you had gone thirty-one seconds longer you would have lost your chance, for, as I have told you before, I had allowed you only sixty seconds in which to say 'yes' or 'no'. I purposely keyed up the requirements, in your case, by allowing you only a brief time in which to decide. This was done because of the tremendous amount of 'sticking' qualities needed to do the sort of job I had laid out for you. I have learned from experience that a man's endurance, or 'sticking' qualities, can be measured in exact ratio to his reaction time in making up his mind to undertake a job.

HILL:

From your remarks, I conclude that organised thinking calls for definiteness of decision as well as action.

CARNEGIE:

That's the idea! Life is short, at best. Time flies in a hurry. An important part of self-discipline is that of developing the habit of quick and definite decisions, always, on every subject. The man who hesitates, when he has all the necessary information before him to enable him to reach a decision, will never get anywhere. He will find himself outmoded by faster thinkers. Right here you will find one of the major differences between men who succeed and men who fail. The man who succeeds often has less ability, less education, less experience than the man who fails, but he has more action consciousness.

HILL:

As I listen to what you say, Mr. Carnegie, I am impressed more and more with the thought that success is more a matter of right mental attitude than it is education.

CARNEGIE:

That is my contention, exactly! Not all the education a man can acquire in a lifetime can take the place of definite, decisive action! If one's thinking does not produce that sort of action, then you may be sure his thinking is not organised.

Organised thought is something like the water in a dam. Only that portion of the water which is harnessed and directed over the wheel is beneficial. The water that pours aimlessly over the dam turns no wheels, performs no service. It just drifts back to the sea.

Every man has a reservoir of thought power, but most men allow this power to be dissipated through idle dreaming, never taking the time to harness it and direct it toward definite ends. Like the water in a dam, it pours over the dam, dissipating its power without performing any service.

HILL:

Why, Mr. Carnegie, do so few men learn to harness and use their thought power? From all you have said about organised thinking I see nothing difficult about it, but there must be some fundamental reason why the vast majority of the people go through life in poverty and misery, without using the power that would give them everything they need or desire.

CARNEGIE:

There is but one major reason for this, and I can state it in one sentence, lack of definiteness of purpose! Most people drift through life, accepting whatever they can get without drawing on the forces of their minds. Lack of a Definite Major Purpose is the most deadly form of self-limitation. It has been plainly written in the records of men that all who demand something definite find ways and means of getting it if they persist in their demands. An important part of persistence is action – the sort of action I have been talking about; action in making a start; action in keeping on going, even when the going is hard; action in making a new start when one is temporarily defeated. Action, action, action! Let that word burn itself into your consciousness until it stands out like the shining sun on a cloudless day.

What you are, what you become, what you acquire, all are the results of your action. Thinking, education, knowledge, native ability, opportunity are nothing but empty words unless they are translated into action. Remember this, and emphasise it throughout the philosophy of individual achievement. Never allow any student of this philosophy to pass under your influence without having the word ACTION burned into his consciousness, for it is one of the key words of the entire philosophy.

The man who leads the entire sales organisation of one of the largest life insurance companies is one of the youngest men on the staff. He has been selling life insurance less than one-fourth the time that other salesmen have worked for the company; he has less personality than the majority of the other salesmen; he knows less about life insurance than many of the others, but he has one thing that gives him top position in sales production, and that is an indomitable will and a whirlwind of action which they do not possess.

And here is how he expresses his action consciousness: When he makes a sale, he induces the buyer to give him a list of other prospective buyers of insurance. He also often manages to get his clients to go with him in person and introduce him to their friends. I think his superior sales record rests almost, if not entirely, upon this one action feat. You see, he forms his clients into an endless chain of cooperative effort, and has, in effect, a large group of men assisting him in selling without having them on his payroll.

HILL:

Why do the other salesmen not profit by this man's example and do likewise?

CARNEGIE:

If I could answer that question, I would change my name from Carnegie to Solomon, and set myself up as an unraveler of human problems. Your question is one that has occurred to me many times, not only in connection with this particular life insurance salesman and his fellow salesmen, but also in relation to my own organisation. It is a well-known fact that certain of my associate workers have risen from the ranks of the humblest sort of labour we perform, and have become principals in the business. The methods by which they promoted themselves are well known to every worker. The major principle that has entered into their promotion is that of Going the Extra Mile. Yet, the percentage of men who have chosen to promote themselves by this simple procedure has been negligible!

In the final analysis, it all goes back to that principle of definiteness of purpose.

The life insurance salesman sells more insurance than any of the others because he wills to do so. That is his Definite Major Purpose and he works at it incessantly. The others work with less willpower, with less definiteness of purpose. Why they do this is something which even they probably cannot explain. They simply lack the necessary urge. Their desires are less obsessional.

HILL:

From your remarks, I conceive that self-discipline is an important factor in a man's achievements.

CARNEGIE:

Of course! The life insurance salesman who leads the entire staff disciplines himself through definitely established habits of action. He makes calls when other salesmen play golf. He sells life insurance when other salesmen are asleep. He has his time definitely budgeted, and he follows the budget schedule with strict self-discipline. I tell you this, although I have never seen the man. And I can tell you another important fact concerning him. He has made the business of selling life insurance an obsession. I doubt not that his subconscious mind goes right on selling insurance while he is asleep, for I have heard it said that on one occasion, he got out of bed, late at night, and telephoned a prospective buyer of insurance, asking for the privilege of conveying the 'prospect' to a convention he knew the prospect desired to attend the next morning. He said nothing about selling life insurance, but he had that ultimate end definitely in mind. Rendering his prospective buyer a favour was but the first step of a definite plan to sell him insurance. You see, when a man charges his mind with this sort of an obsession, his subconscious mind takes over his obsession and aids him in translating it into its physical or financial equivalent.

HILL:

Obsessional desire, then, is also an important part of organised thinking?

CARNEGIE:

Yes, a very important part! As a matter of fact, it is the part which starts action and keeps action going. A man has no difficulty in doing that which he desires to do. Obsessional desire comes to a man's rescue in times of defeat, through unforeseen emergencies, and aids him in making a new start without the loss of confidence in himself. It keeps him moving when otherwise he would yield to the habit of procrastination. It takes the drudgery out of his labour.

HILL:

And this brings us back, again, to the question of 'mental

attitude' based on motive. Obsessional desire is a mental attitude one can acquire if one has a definite motive back of the desire. Is that the idea?

CARNEGIE:

You've stated it perfectly. 'Mental attitude' represents the sum total of one's emotional feelings at any given time. Through self-discipline, a man can determine which of his emotions will have the fullest expression and which of them will be modified, controlled and redirected through transmutation. Mental attitude is controlled through established habits based on definite motives. Here, again, enters the question of action. Habits of control over mental attitude can be established only by appropriate expression of the emotions, through physical action.

HILL:

Suppose a man is lacking in ambition, and has a weak imagination. How can he be induced to overcome these weaknesses?

CARNEGIE:

In your question you have, consciously or otherwise, described the actual condition of the majority of people. Lack of ambition stands near the head of the list of causes of failure. There is no hope of success for such a person until he has been fired with sufficient ambition to cause him to want something he does not possess. Desire based on a definite motive is, as we have stated many times, the beginning of all achievements. And right here I wish to call your attention to an important fact we have not mentioned previously, namely that every successful person owes his success, in a large measure, to the influence of some other person who crossed his life somewhere and somehow.

Take your own case, for example. You came to interview me for the purpose of writing a story about my personal achievements. Before you were through with the interview I influenced you to change your entire plan of life, give up your aim of becoming a lawyer, and give the world a practical philosophy of individual achievement.

In a similar manner, every successful man comes under the influence of some other person who fires his imagination with an idea that becomes obsessional with him. Sometimes the source of this outside inspiration is attained by remote control, through the reading of a book. But always there is a turning point in every successful person's life which marks the place at which he came under the influence of another mind that inspired him with higher aims and nobler purposes.

Very often, successful men lose sight of the original source of their inspiration, and not infrequently do they forget it conveniently because they prefer to have the world believe their achievements to be of their own doing entirely.

HILL:

That is an entirely new thought, Mr. Carnegie, but I can see that it is sound. Then is it not true that an important part of organised thinking consists in one's deliberate efforts to associate with those who are capable of inspiring him with higher and nobler aims?

CARNEGIE:

Yes, and I might add that the wise man never wastes his time with anyone from whom he cannot acquire benefits or to whom he cannot contribute something worthwhile in one form or another. Personal associations are important, because everyone acquires something of the philosophy, the personality, and the mental attitude of those with whom he associates closely. As I have stated, there is a law of nature which controls this.

HILL:

By the self-same rule, is it not also true that many of a man's destructive qualities, such as a negative mental attitude, are acquired from association with others?

CARNEGIE:

Yes, that is true. I have never yet heard of a young person getting into serious trouble that did not grow out of his association with undesirable characters. Human associations are much more responsible for one's success or failure in life than most people believe them to be. No wise person would anymore form close friendships with people with negative minds than one would drink water from a well he knew to be contaminated with disease germs. Human traits are contagious, both the good and the bad.

HILL:

As you unfold this subject of organised thinking, Mr. Carnegie, there seems to be no end to the conditions and circumstances that enter into it.

CARNEGIE:

That is right. The conditions which influence organised thinking are, in fact, as numerous as are the facts which enter into all human intercourse. Every word a man speaks, every word spoken in his presence, every thought a man thinks, modifies his thinking habits in one way or another. Naturally, if a man jockeys himself into such a relationship with others that he associates only with those who inspire him to think noble thoughts and engage in commendable deeds, he benefits by improving the nature of his own thoughts. The reverse is true if by carelessness or indifference he allows himself to drift into the company of people whose minds are negative.

HILL:

Then you wouldn't say it was selfish for a man to refuse to associate with any except those from whom he can gain some sort of benefit or contribute something worthwhile?

CARNEGIE:

That might be called selfishness, but it is a justifiable form of selfishness. No matter by what name it is called; it is essential for success through organised thinking. A man does not hesitate to demand the best food he can get for his physical body, although he may know there are people who are in want of even the coarsest of food. Why, therefore, should a man be less careful about the food he feeds his mind? And make no mistake about it: Every influence that reaches a man through his association with others constitutes mental food for his mind. I have seen tramps fishing discarded food from swill barrels, but I have also seen men who were not tramps fishing 'mental food' from the minds of their associates which was far more detrimental to their well-being than would be the discarded food from a swill barrel. This is not a pretty simile, but it is accurate.

HILL:

When you speak of daily associates, do you have reference to a man's business or social associates?

CARNEGIE:

I have reference to all his associates with whom he enters into friendly intercourse. Listed in the order of their importance from the viewpoint of the influence a man's associates have on him I would say that his family associates come first, then his business or occupational associates, then his social friends, and lastly his casual associates. No relationship is as important as that of a man's family associates. Here is where most men are made or unmade, according to the nature of their home relationships. This relationship exercises a powerful influence in a man's life, and it begins at birth and continues all through life. That old saying that a man can be made or broken by the influence of his wife is true in all but a few rare cases where a man is strong enough to throw off the influence of a negative wife. On the other hand a clever wife can, and often she does, inspire her husband to aim higher and achieve the object of his aim. Fortunate, indeed, is the man who selects a wife whose influence on him is inspiring and constructive.

HILL:

Of course, you have not intentionally overlooked mentioning a man's Master Mind associates as being an important factor in his business or occupational achievements. Would these not come before all other influences?

CARNEGIE:

As far as one's business achievements are concerned, yes. But, if you have reference to a man's success as a whole, I still say that his family relationships come first, because here is where a man has his more intimate relationships, and it is these that make or disrupt his peace of mind. The ideal relationship, of course, is one in which a man's wife (if he is married) becomes also a member of his Master Mind alliance. She may not participate in the business conferences he has with the other members of his alliance, but she can have a lot to do with the 'Mental attitude' in which he enters these conferences, and in that way exercise a powerful influence on the group as a whole that affect him.

HILL:

You emphasise the importance of knowing well your Master Mind allies. You go on the theory, I suppose, that an enemy recognised is an enemy half controlled?

CARNEGIE:

Yes, and you might add that if you know a great deal about your enemies you stand a fair chance of being able to convert them into friends. The habit of underrating one's enemies, or competitors, is a costly habit. No organised thinker indulges in such costly mistakes. The organised thinker accepts as grist everything that comes to his mill, but he takes care to separate the wheat from the chaff in the grinding process. The chaff can be converted into useful service if it is recognised and classified.

HILL:

Meaning, by your simile, just what, Mr. Carnegie?

CARNEGIE:

Well, I'll give you an illustration of exactly what I mean. I once had a close business associate whose home life became dangerously disturbed by his interests in another woman. This man's wife came to me with her story and asked my aid in breaking up the affair. I went right to work on it, not by mentioning the affair to my associate, but dealing indirectly with the woman in the case.

Inside of a month, I had convinced the woman of the inappropriateness of the whole affair, and of the damage it was destined to do my business associate if it were not discontinued. The details I cannot mention, but suffice it to say that the home relationship of my associate was satisfactorily restored, thereby saving embarrassment to many people. If I had ignored the facts when they were first called to my attention, I would eventually have lost an able business associate, and his wife would have lost a fine husband. By using common sense and working together, under the principle of organised thinking, his wife and I averted what would otherwise have become a tragedy.

HILL:

Oh! I see what you mean. Organised thinking makes it

necessary for a man to depart from his regular routine when emergencies, such as the one you have related, threaten to interfere with the attainment of his own goal in life. Is that the idea, Mr. Carnegie?

CARNEGIE:

That is just what I mean. It was not my responsibility to interfere with my business associate's private life, but it was my privilege to do so, and I acted on that privilege in what I considered the best interest of all concerned.

HILL:

Suppose that your efforts to deal with the woman in this case had not been successful. Would you have given up the matter?

CARNEGIE:

The organised thinker never gives up anything he undertakes until he has exhausted every effort to finish it, and you may put that down as another essential of organised thinking. No, if my first effort had failed, I would have tried another plan, and still another. As a last resort, I might have disassociated myself from my associate until he learned the error of his ways, then have made a new alliance with him. Every problem has a solution of some sort, although it may not always be the solution one would like. The trouble with people who do not organise their thinking is that they give up and quit when they run into opposition. Quitting never solved any problem.

HILL:

Then persistence is also an important factor in organised thinking?

CARNEGIE:

Indeed it is. As a matter of fact, 'persistence' is a key word in all forms of individual achievement. Without it, no one can go very far in any undertaking. Persistence takes its place along with action. The two are inseparable.

HILL:

How may one acquire persistence, Mr. Carnegie?

CARNEGIE:

By developing the power of the will. Persistence is nothing

but an indomitable will, plus a definite motive to inspire action. Bring together these three factors – motive, action, and willpower – and they result in what we call persistence.

HILL:

I suppose one develops the power of will in the same manner by expressing a definite desire, or motive, in terms of action.

CARNEGIE:

Yes, the power of will responds only to motive, but it becomes stronger the more it is used. When a man takes possession of his own willpower, he has all the other faculties of his mind under his control, for it is the boss of them all.

Hill:

Then one cannot become an organised thinker without gaining control of his willpower. Is that correct?

CARNEGIE:

That is precisely correct. And do not forget that the will responds to controlled habits, based on definite motives, which is the same as saying that the way to gain control of the will is by developing action habits that are related to the exercise of the will.

HILL:

Thank you, Mr. Carnegie, for explaining the elements and importance of Organised Thought in such detail.

> EVERY student of this philosophy should have the word ACTION burned into his consciousness, for it is one of the key words of the entire philosophy.
>
> —Andrew Carnegie
>
> IF YOU cannot get that which you want, you can change your desires and want something you can get.
>
> IF YOU wish to know the "motive" which inspires one to concentrate his mind on a definite purpose, observe the actions of those who are in love. Obsessional desire, based on intense emotion, is the source of all genius.

□

CHAPTER THREE
Controlled Attention

Hidden in the two words 'Controlled Attention' is a strange power that is sufficient to remove all the ordinary self-imposed limitations which people accept, and by which they are bound throughout their lives.

The power is literally 'mental dynamite', as it is capable of blasting the cause of self-imposed limitations, and giving one the means by which he may take charge of his own mind.

When you master this chapter, you will understand more fully why one must have a Definite Major Purpose in order to attain success. You will know, also, why one's Definite Major Purpose should be written out, memorised, and repeated often. You will understand why one's 'Mental attitude' plays such an important part in carrying out the object of one's major purpose, or any minor purpose.

The subject of Controlled Attention is the basis of many sects and religions, although it may be called by other names. It has been the major weapon used by powerful military leaders, some of whom have not always made constructive use of it.

Through this chapter, we shall get a better understanding of the Master Mind principle, the results of which have baffled men of science and astounded laymen who have witnessed its operations.

The alliance of two or more minds, working in perfect harmony for the attainment of a definite purpose, has the effect of stimulating the mind of each person in the alliance, and results in providing the members of the alliance, or some individual in the group, with a source of knowledge that sometimes cannot be traced to the accumulated knowledge of any of the individuals.

This result we are familiar with, because it is a result that is taking place in the research laboratories and the business and industrial councils throughout the world, almost as a daily routine. We see evidence on every hand that such a combination of minds gives men vision, courage, imagination, and initiative which they do not possess when they act independently and alone, and we know that this power is available even to men whose avowed purpose in its use is the destruction of the best that civilisation has given the world.

Andrew Carnegie included the principle of Controlled Attention as one of the principles of individual achievement, but even the great steel master failed to associate this principle with the means by which civilisation may be advanced. He saw in it a power that is adaptable to one's needs in the solution of economic and personal problems of a material nature, but beyond this point, he made no mention of its possibilities.

Mr. Carnegie readily acknowledged that his huge fortune was accumulated solely through the efforts of a combination of minds consisting of some twenty men who were allied with him as a Master Mind group, for the purpose of making and marketing steel. He acquired the technique necessary to induce those men to work with him in a spirit of harmony. He knew that the creative vision, imagination, initiative, and inspiration produced through this Master Mind alliance were great, but he made no attempt to explain the source of the super power they gave him.

Since Mr. Carnegie first brought this principle to my attention, more than a quarter of a century of intense research into the causes of its power has been carried on. The minds of thousands of people have been explored, their reactions to thought stimuli have been examined, and conclusions have been reached which may be of utmost importance to this and future generations, in the matter of adjustment of human relationships.

Come with me now, for a brief elementary lesson in organic chemistry, for here is where we find the first convincing clue to what happens when two or more minds are blended, in a spirit of harmony, for the attainment of a single purpose.

In chemistry, we learn that two or more elements of an entirely different nature can be so combined that they produce something different from either of the elements. For illustration, water, which is known in chemistry as H_2O, is a compound consisting of two parts of hydrogen and one atom of oxygen, but the result is neither oxygen nor hydrogen. This marrying of the elements produces an entirely new product.

We also learn in chemistry that certain harmless drugs can be so compounded that they become deadly poisonous, while still other combinations of drugs, added to the poison, will neutralize its poisonous effect.

Throughout nature, we see that every atom of matter and every unit of energy is definitely modified by its nearest associates. Vegetation, the things that grow out of the ground, are definitely modified by the elements of the soil on which they feed, a fact that is well known to every farmer and every horticulturist. Yes, the atoms of matter are influenced by the presence of their 'neighbours', the same as people are. The world in which we live and the material portion of the universe which we can observe are made up of electrons, which, in final analysis, consist of positive and negative units of energy so arranged that the two forces balance each other and are practically inseparable by any method known to science.

The material portion of the universe consists, as far as science has been able to determine the facts, of only two things, energy and matter. And it appears, if one wishes to be strictly technical in the statement of facts, that the so-called material portion of the universe is nothing but energy, since obviously the electrons of matter are known to be nothing but two opposing forms of energy, one 'pushing' and the other 'pulling' in such a manner as to neutralise their combined energy.

Taking our cue from the chemistry of matter we come, now, to the analysis of the power of thought. Obviously, thought is energy, and for all that science has learned about it, or its cause, it may be precisely the same sort of energy that holds the opposing forces of the electron together. If that is true, then it is clear that the energy of thought responds to the same modifying influences that change the nature of the elements of matter, one of which, as we have seen, is the manner in which the atoms of matter are combined.

There are two facts of which we are sure. First, that the nature of matter can be changed by combining the elements of other matter, and second, that the nature of thought can be modified and changed by the alliance of two or more minds, and this despite the nature of the alliance, or for what purpose it is made. These are facts so well known, even to laymen, that they are readily accepted as such.

We know that there are certain types of minds which, when they contact each other through any sort of intercourse, become definitely antagonistic to each other. In this circumstance, we find a reasonable hypothesis for the belief that the chemistry of the brain and the chemistry of matter in other fields, are the same; that the same law of nature which changes harmless chemical elements into deadly poison, by the mere act of combining them, changes also the vibrations of thought, when mixed in certain combinations, to an antagonising influence.

In other words, there are certain combinations of thought energy which 'fight' the moment they come into contact with each other. Nor is this fact demonstrable alone in the relationship of two or more individuals; it can also be seen in the operations of an individual mind, for it is well known that there are types of thought which 'repel' as soon as they come together. The emotion of fear and the emotion of faith, for example, are so unfriendly that both cannot possibly occupy the brain at the same time. One or the other must, and it always does, dominate. There are certain means by which an individual may determine which of these two emotions, or any other emotions, shall dominate his brain, and one of the more important of these methods is Controlled Attention.

As a part of this description, I must now call attention to a law of nature through which like attracts like. We sometimes call this law the law of harmonious attraction. Through its operation, things that are suited to one another, in the great scheme of life, have a natural tendency to get together.

We see this law in operation in connection with vegetation that grows from the soil. Through some strange and unknown process, this law manages to bring together the chemical elements of the soil and combine them with the units of energy of the elements of the air so as to produce every living thing that grows from the ground. Here there is no antagonism, no 'fighting' among the elements of matter or the units of energy. They do their work in response to the law of harmonious attraction, without opposition among themselves.

When we come to the relationship between men, we find another situation through which the law of harmonious attraction is often disregarded, and unfriendly forces of thought energy break up relationships of harmony. Sometimes this happens because of man's ignorance of the law of harmonious attraction; sometimes it is the result of man's deliberate substitution of negative thoughts which are known to be destructive of the influence of the law of harmonious attraction.

The person who has mastered this philosophy and has formed the habit of applying it in all his relationships with other people finds himself benefited by the law of harmonious attraction. He has conditioned his brain to attract to himself only such people and material things as he desires. Now let us see how he goes about the process of conditioning his brain so as to enable him to adapt himself to the influence of the law of harmonious attraction, viz.:

1. DEFINITENESS OF PURPOSE: He decides precisely what he wants, lays out a plan for acquiring it, and then proceeds to concentrate the major portion of his thoughts and deeds on that end, following his thoughts with appropriate physical action. Here, then, enters the principle of Controlled Attention, and let us not overlook the fact that this has the effect of giving him the benefit of the law of harmonious attraction, in two different ways. First, he attracts the forces of a positive mental attitude which create harmony within his own mind. Second, he attracts people and material things which harmonise with the nature of his purpose.

Through Controlled Attention, and by that method alone, may one impress the nature of his desires, aims, and plans upon his subconscious mind, where the law of harmonious attraction appears to find contact with them.

2. THE MASTER MIND: Having made the first step in the development of the habit of Controlled Attention, by the adoption of a Definite Major Purpose, he must form a Master Mind alliance with others who have the necessary experience, education, native ability, and who have been supplied with the necessary motive, to help attain the object of his major purpose.

This Master Mind relationship intensifies the application of the principle of Controlled Attention, because the alliance creates a powerful 'mass psychology' which gives one increased self-reliance, imagination, enthusiasm, initiative and the will to win. A man will keep on moving in the direction of his Definite Major Purpose when he is associated with others who lend him aid and encouragement, whereas he would be inclined to slow down, and to divert his attention from his major objective, if he worked alone.

The Master Mind alliance, when it is keyed up and actively engaged in carrying out some definite objective, is Controlled Attention in its highest form! Such an alliance keeps one continuously reminded of his purpose in life; particularly where one is associated daily with the members of his Master Mind group, as are the successful leaders of industrial and business organisations.

3. APPLIED FAITH: The man who has adopted a Definite Major Purpose, and has surrounded himself with a group of other people, in a Master Mind alliance, and is actively engaged in carrying out the object of his alliance, thereby demonstrates his faith in his ability to attain his objective. Therefore, the element of faith enters into his application of the principle of Controlled Attention, thus further intensifying his power of concentration. By the time this third step has been taken, in developing the habit of controlled Attention, one's mental attitude has become predominantly positive; many of the self-imposed limitations of doubt and discouragement and lack of self-reliance have disappeared; one moves with definiteness in all he does; he has no room left in his mind for thoughts of failure; he is so busily engaged in carrying out the object of his

major purpose that he has no time to hesitate or procrastinate; moreover, he has no desire to do so.

The third step in the development of Controlled Attention would be sufficient to ensure success, in a majority of cases, but the master of this philosophy does not stop here. He proceeds to 'freeze' the gains he has made by taking the fourth step:

4. GOING THE EXTRA MILE: The application of this principle ensures continuous action. It brings into operation the principle of increasing returns through which one's efforts are greatly multiplied. It creates an added momentum behind one's efforts which inspires both the individual and his Master Mind associates, as well as others who are definitely related to the object of his Definite Major Purpose. It also serves to modify his mental attitude by making it more positive. While it may not bring him direct material benefits on every occasion that this principle is applied, it has the general effect of creating goodwill and attracting the cooperation of others, in a spirit of friendliness. Thus it serves as fuel to feed the fire of Controlled Attention!

But this is not the stopping point! The master of this philosophy further ensures his successful attainment of the object of his Definite Major Purpose by taking the fifth step in the development of the habit of Controlled Attention:

5. Organised INDIVIDUAL ENDEAVOR: Through the application of this principle one organizes his plans, then, with the aid of his Master Mind allies he analyses his plans, tests them, and makes sure that they are sound. By this time he has established a sound reason for his faith; therefore he moves with self-assurance that practically defies opposition! He is no longer held back by indecision and doubt. He knows precisely what he wants, he has definite plans for acquiring what he wants, and he is actively engaged in carrying out his plans, flanked and aided by Master Mind allies in whom he has confidence, and who, in turn, inspire him with greater confidence in himself and his plans. But, he does not stop here. He takes the sixth step in consolidating his gains, by applying another important principle of this philosophy, viz.:

6. SELF-DISCIPLINE: Through the aid of this principle, the emotions are harnessed and brought under control. He no longer dissipates his energies, either by the overindulgence of his positive emotions or by giving expression to his negative emotions. His mind begins to function like a perfectly constructed piece of machinery, with no lost motion, no dissipation of energy. He has acquired the art of transmutation of his emotions; therefore his negative emotions (if and when they present themselves to his mind) are converted into positive action.

He has begun to acquire complete control over his faculty of will, with the aid of which all the other departments of the mind are brought under his control and made to do constructive duty. He is approaching the apex of efficiency in the art of Controlled Attention. From here on, he has everything under control, but there are still other steps to be taken which put the finishing touches on the consolidation of his gains over himself and the circumstances of his life which affect his attainment of his Definite Major Purpose. Moving more swiftly now, because of the gains he has made through the six steps he has taken, he takes the seventh step, viz.:

7. CREATIVE VISION: By the time the previous six steps have been taken, the faculty of imagination will have become so keen and alert that it begins to function automatically, thus further consolidating one's efforts to develop the habit of Controlled Attention. By this time, the subconscious mind will have swung into action on its own account, and it will have begun to express itself through plans and ideas that will appear in the form of 'hunches'. New opportunities will begin mysteriously to appear, and new and unexpected forms of cooperation from others will begin to present themselves. Everything he touches will appear to become a tool placed in his hands with which he may promote the object of his Definite Major Purpose. Even the law of chance will appear to be operating in his favour. His friends will begin to speak of him as one who is blessed by 'luck'. But, let no one be deceived on this point. Back of these favourable circumstances what will appear from all directions is a definite cause, and the master of this

philosophy will understand that this 'cause' may be explained by the application of the seven principles here mentioned.

But, the person who has mastered this entire philosophy will not be content to rest on his oars at this point. He will proceed to further consolidate his gains in the development of Controlled Attention by taking the eighth step.

8. ORGANISED THOUGHT: Long before this point will have been reached, the master of this philosophy will have stopped 'guessing', and he will have formed the habit of building plans based on known facts, or reasonable hypotheses of facts. As a matter of fact, he will have begun, simultaneously with the adoption of a Definite Major Purpose, to organise his thinking.

By no means should it be assumed that he will wait until he has taken the eighth step in the development of Controlled Attention to apply the principle of Organised Thought. At this point, however, this principle will have become obviously a necessity in the development of the habit of Controlled Attention. Remember, we are now talking about the habit of Controlled Attention, the foundation for which must be laid by the application of Organised Thought beginning with the adoption of a Definite Major Purpose.

9. LEARNING FROM DEFEAT: By this time, the student of this philosophy will have acquired the habit of converting every experience of his life into some definite benefit. Defeat will have become nothing but a signal for greater and more determined effort. He will have acquired the habit of searching for the 'seed of an equivalent benefit' that is to be found in all forms of defeat. Defeat, therefore, will become a form of useful fuel with which he feeds the fire of his own willpower. He will not only convert current defeats into an urge to greater endeavour, but he will have acquired the habit of going back into his memory and profiting by all his previous defeats. This he will accomplish by taking retrospective inventory of himself every few months, thus enabling himself to analyse defeat from its results, through the lapse of time sufficient to remove the sting of the experience.

By this time, the master of this philosophy will have become literally a 'giant' of power, compared with his former self, and there will be no space left in his brain for the housing of fear, discouragement, worry, or self-limitations of any other nature. He will know what he wants and where he is going in life, and he will recognise that he is well on his way toward his destination. The road ahead of him will be clear, and although it may have many curves beyond which he cannot see, he will know that when he reaches these, the road will continue onward towards his destination. This is a glorious feeling, as every person who has experienced noteworthy achievement can testify.

Having learned the art of converting defeat into a stimulus for greater effort, the student of this philosophy goes the tenth step in the development of Controlled Attention:

10. INSPIRATION: The gains attained through the application of the nine principles here described lead to the development of the habit of enthusiasm, the action producing quality that inspires one to take the initiative instead of being told what to do. The Inspired Feeling of enthusiasm takes the drudgery out of work and converts one's physical action into a pleasant experience, thus simplifying the development of Controlled Attention. Enthusiasm in connection with any plan, purpose, or motive automatically leads to the concentration of attention upon that subject. Through the principle of inspiration, the dominating thoughts of one's mind are quickly impressed, upon the subconscious mind, where they are acted upon; thus the person whose mind is dominated by enthusiasm has the direct support of what is assumed to be the connecting link between the conscious mind and Infinite Intelligence. At this point, he has attained a high degree of efficiency in the application of Controlled Attention.

Meanwhile, the master of this philosophy will have added momentum to his efforts, in support of the ten principles here described, by the application of the eleventh principle, through which he will taken the next step in developing the habit of Controlled Attention, viz.:

11. ATTRACTIVE PERSONALITY: While this is mentioned as the eleventh step in the development of the habit of Controlled Attention, the student will have begun applying this principle immediately following his adoption of a Definite Major Purpose. By application of the qualities of an Attractive Personality, he

will have removed much of the opposition of other people, and he will have attracted the friendly cooperation of many allies other than those allied with him in his Master Mind group. He will have, also, improved his own mental attitude, thus preparing the way for the development of any desired habit, including the habit of Controlled Attention.

It is obvious, therefore, that Controlled Attention is the result of the application of all the principles here mentioned, and not a matter of chance. It is obvious, also, that the method by which the habit of Controlled Attention is developed involves no effort beyond the ability of the average person; it calls for no special training or education other than that here mentioned; it is a success quality well within the reach of the person of average ability; its development calls for no unreasonable amount of sacrifice or labor, the major requirements being the will to win and a willingness to pay the price of achievement in terms of honest application.

Having mastered these eleven principles, through systematic application and use, the student of this philosophy finds himself pushed forward into the twelfth and last step in the development of the habit of Controlled Attention. In mastering the eleven principles he has automatically developed the twelfth, and lo! he finds himself the master of himself, the 'master of his fate, the captain of his soul!'

Although only twelve of the principles of this philosophy have been considered, the person who has mastered these is now in possession of his own mind. He knows what he wants. He has a plan for acquiring it. He has surrounded himself with trustworthy aids in acquiring the object of his Definite Major Purpose. He feels the thrill of personal power. He has the necessary self-discipline to enable him to use this power wisely; nay, he has no desire to use it in any other than a constructive manner that benefits all whom it influences.

He has become a constructive unit of the great American way of life, and as such he has given himself immunity against the subtle forces seeking to destroy the American form of self-determination and personal freedom. He has learned how to acquire his needs without damaging others. He no longer desires something for nothing, for he has learned a better way of acquiring his needs. He has found peace and harmony within his own mind. He has learned to accept the circumstances of life as he finds them and to make the most of them. He has acquired the art of peaceful and harmonious negotiation with others through which he relates himself to other people in a manner that works for the good of all.

Let us now give attention to another feature of Controlled Attention, which suggests the way to personal power, through a combination of principles.

As I have stated, there is a chemistry of the brain through which the mind power of individuals is modified by the influence of one mind on another. This fact is obvious, even to the layman who has given no particular study to the subject of mental phenomena or personalities.

We have seen, also, that in the field of organic chemistry, certain harmless elements may be so combined as to create a deadly poison. From these observations, we may safely assume that everything, from the individual atom of matter to a human being, is modified or changed in some form by the presence of other things.

Knowing these facts to be such, we shall have no difficulty in assuming that the presence, in the mind, of a combination of thoughts may convert them into a power that cannot be identified with any individual thought, and one that may be greater than all of them combined.

For example, we know from observation and experience that the following principles, when assembled in the mind through a combination of thoughts, may produce mind power bordering upon the 'miraculous':

(a) Definiteness of Purpose
(b) Self-discipline, through control of the emotions
(c) Controlled Attention
(d) Autosuggestion, applied to the object of one's purpose
(e) The power of will, actively engaged

Here is a combination of principles capable of producing sufficient power for the solution of almost any problem by which one is confronted. The power comes from the combination, not from any single principle. Let us see how the principles are applied to produce power:

Let us say that a man is faced by one of the commonest of all problems, the need of a certain amount of money for some specific purpose, within a specified time. There are two major ways of dealing with the problem. First, by worrying about it but doing nothing to raise the money. This is the usual way of handling such problems. Second, by combining the five principles here mentioned and going after the money in earnest.

The amount of money required is known and one has made up his mind to get it. That is definiteness of purpose.

The mind is put to work (through the faculty of the imagination) acquiring the money, to the exclusion of all other problems. That is Controlled Attention.

The mind is cleared of all fear and doubt that the money cannot be procured. That is self-discipline. The control of the emotion of fear thus prepares the mind for the exercise of faith.

The mind is put to work (through the faculty of the imagination) on creating something of an equivalent value that is to be given in return for the money, or for its temporary use, and it is kept at work until it singles out one specific idea. That is autosuggestion.

The mind is given repeated suggestions that the amount of money desired will be procured, no matter what the cost may be or what conditions have to be complied with, and there it remains, set, determined, persistent. That is willpower, in action.

> LINCOLN'S MIND was like a piece of steel – very hard to scratch anything on it and almost impossible, after you get it on, to rub it out.

When these five principles are combined, and applied in the manner described with variations to suit each different circumstance, the subconscious mind goes to work and creates a plan – sometimes a variety of plans – by which the money may be procured.

If one experiences failure, it is because there has been a slackening of effort in connection with one or more of these principles. I have seen this combination of principles produce results that were almost unbelievable. I have heard highly successful men endorse this combination of principles as having super power which they made no effort to explain because it seems inexplicable.

The combination of the five principles I have just mentioned provides one with power that is not attributable to any one of these principles alone. The experiences of men of great achievement bear this out. First we shall hear from Thomas A. Edison, whose statement on the subject is quoted as nearly verbatim as memory will permit:

'You ask me,' said Mr. Edison, "to name the most important essential in the field of invention. Well, I can describe it very briefly. It consists, first, of definite knowledge as to what one wants to achieve [definiteness of purpose]. One must fix his mind on that purpose with that sort of persistence which knows no such word as 'impossible', and begin searching for that which he seeks, making use of all the accumulated knowledge on the subject he can find, drawing upon his own experience, and making use of the experience of other people [the Master Mind, Controlled Attention, autosuggestion]. He must keep on searching, no matter how many times his search leads to a dead end street [power of will]. He must refuse to be influenced by the fact that someone else may have tried the same idea without success [self-discipline, mastery of fear and doubt]. He must keep himself 'sold' on the idea that the solution of his problem exists somewhere, and that he will find it [autosuggestion]."

Then Mr. Edison went on to say, "When a man makes up his mind to solve a problem he may, at first, meet with dogged opposition; but if he holds on and keeps searching, he will be sure to find some sort of a solution. I never knew the plan to fail. [A combination of all five of the principles is involved here.] "The trouble with most people," he continued, 'is that they quit before they start.' By this, he meant, of course, that self-imposed limitations prohibit most people from beginning tasks which they might easily complete if they made a start and kept on going, in the right sort of mental attitude.

'In all my experience,' Mr. Edison said, "I do not recall ever having found the solution to any problem connected with invention through my first effort, with the exception of the talking machine. And one of the most surprising of all things is the fact that when I have discovered that for which I am searching, I generally find that the answer was within my reach all the time, but nothing but persistence and a will to win would have uncovered it."

Now let us hear from Dr. Alexander Graham Bell, the inventor of the modern telephone.

"I discovered the principle of the long distance telephone while searching for the means of producing a mechanical hearing aid, for the benefit of my wife whose hearing was impaired. I made up my mind to find that for which I was searching if it required the remainder of my life. After innumerable failures, I finally uncovered the principle for which I was searching, and was astounded at its simplicity. I was still more astounded to discover that the principle I revealed was not only beneficial in the construction of a mechanical hearing aid, but it served also as a means of sending the sound of the voice over a wire."

Dr. Bell made use of all five of the principles here described, although he may have done so unconsciously. "Another discovery that grew out of my investigations," said Dr. Bell, "was the fact that when a man gives his brain an order to produce a definite result, and stands by that order, it seems to have the effect of giving him a 'second sight' that enables him to see right through ordinary problems. What this power is I cannot say; all I know is that it exists, and it becomes available only when a man is in that state of mind in which he knows exactly what he wants and is determined to get just that."

I shall now introduce John Wanamaker, the late "merchant king of Philadelphia".

"On numerous occasions during the early part of my business career," said Mr. Wanamaker, "I found myself in need of funds for the operation of my business, which I could not procure through any of the usual commercial or banking channels. On every such occasion, I made it my business to go out to the park and begin walking, thinking as I walked of new sources of approach to the solution of my problem. On one such occasion, I needed a very large sum, due to the fact that we had an off season and found our shelves stocked with merchandise we could not convert into ready cash. I made up my mind not to go back to the store until I had solved my problem. I kept my mind on it every second! At the end of about the second hour, an idea burst into my mind that enabled me to walk right back to the store and raise the necessary amount of money within 15 minutes. The strangest part of the experience was the fact I did not think of that idea at the start."

Controlled attention, plus Definiteness of Purpose, formed the combination that served Mr. Wanamaker in this instance. Perhaps Applied Faith was a part of the combination of principles he used but of that he made no mention. He did say, however, that "I doubt that there is any such reality as an unsolvable problem for the man who has learned how to hold his mind on his problem with a firm determination to find its solution." That was the equivalent to saying that there is no such thing as an unsolvable problem for the man who knows how to use faith.

Now let us hear from Dr. Elmer R. Gates, one of the distinguished scientists and inventors of three decades ago who collaborated in the organisation of this philosophy.

"There is some hidden source of power," said Dr. Gates, "which comes to a man's aid when he sets his mind on a definite goal and becomes determined to attain it. With the aid of this power, I have uncovered the secrets of more than 200 inventions, not one of which existed in my accumulated knowledge at the beginning of my search. It is possible to fix the attention on a given problem and to keep it there until the solution of the problem seems to float into the mind from the air. The greatest of all problems is that of maintaining sufficient will power to keep one's mind concentrated upon a single purpose long enough to enable one to tap this mysterious source of inward sight."

When asked to explain what he meant by the term 'inward sight' Dr. Gates replied, "I have reference to the sixth sense through which the subconscious mind seems to yield the answer to problems submitted to it in the mental attitude I have described."

Remember, these men were among the most distinguished men of achievement known to the people of America during their lifetime. Each was a recognised success in his own field.

Let us have a word now from the late President Woodrow Wilson.

"When the request came from the German military authorities for an armistice, in 1918," said Mr. Wilson, "it presented one of the greatest and most profound problems of my two terms in the White House. I knew a decision had to be made. I knew that the lives of thousands of people depended upon that decision. And I knew that I had to make the decision. I laid the request aside for a few minutes, close my eyes, and became determined to seek guidance from a source greater than my own faculty of reason. In a little while, I picked up the paper and walked out onto the rear porch of the White House, stood there with my eyes closed, the paper clenched in my hand, and asked for Divine guidance. I was resolved not to rely upon my own judgement alone.

In a little while – it was not more than five minutes – the answer came! It was so definite, so obviously sound, that I went right back to my study and wrote the reply in shorthand. Subsequent events proved that I made the right answer, for it was but a little while after I sent it that the German Kaiser had been dethroned by his own people and was on his way into exile."

What was this strange power on which the war President relied for his answer? He made no attempt to explain it! One can only surmise as to what he believed it to be, but there is one fact of which there is no doubt; the President forced his mind to seek the solution of a grave problem and it produced the desired results. His experience was Controlled Attention of the most profound nature.

It appears that Controlled Attention is more effective during an emergency, when one is forced to concentrate his thoughts upon some definite problem. And let it not be forgotten that Controlled Attention has a great deal of power when it is motivated by fear, but the power seems to be limited to the medium of physical expression of power. When frightened, a man may develop great physical strength, because he concentrates all of his efforts in some particular direction, but this sort of power is small indeed, in comparison with the spiritual power that becomes available through the emotion of faith.

Controlled Attention, inspired by faith, is a far different power from that which is created through fear! If Woodrow Wilson had concentrated his mind upon his answer to the German government's request for an armistice in a spirit of fear, I doubt that he would have received the sort of guidance that he did, which enabled him to send an answer that put an end to the former Kaiser of Germany.

Dr. Bell discovered the principle which made the telephone possible as the result of an emergency, occasioned by his wife's deafness. Of course, the significance of the 'emergency' is this: It causes one to control his attention in a more highly concentrate form than he would under ordinary circumstances. It appears that these unexplained results (sometimes called 'miracles') experienced by people who rely upon their own minds, generally occur under the stress of some emergency when by the very nature of the circumstance, they are forced to intensify the concentration of their thoughts upon a definite subject.

Two factors are always present under such circumstances. First, the emergency steps up the vibration of thought to a highly intense state of emotional feeling. Second, that emotion is concentrated upon one Definite Major Purpose!

The purpose of Controlled Attention, as far as this philosophy is concerned, is that of enabling one to bring together all the departments of the mind and harness their combined power for use in connection with a given purpose. That is what controlled attention amounts to. It stimulates coordinated action by (1) the faculty of the will, (2) the faculty of the emotions, (3) the faculty of reason, (4) the conscience, (5) the memory, (6) the faculty of the imagination, (7) the sixth sense, (8) the subconscious section of the mind; and it seems a reasonable hypothesis to assume that the combined forces of these departments of the mind make direct contact with all of them into action simultaneously.

This hypothesis seems all the more logical because it has the endorsement, in about the same terms in which we have described it, of the Late Thomas A. Edison, Dr. Elmer R. Gates, Dr. Alexander Graham Bell, President Woodrow Wilson, Andrew Carnegie, and many others equally capable of reaching a logical conclusion on so profound a subject.

The facts upon which this hypothesis is based, with one exception, are known to be accurate. It is known that the combined power of the eight factors of the mind, when they are coordinated and expressed in action, through Controlled Attention, enables one to perform deeds which border on the 'miraculous'. The source of power that makes this possible has not been isolated definitely, but the results are so astounding that they could not be attributed to any power short of Infinite Intelligence.

The burden of this lesson, however, is not to define the source of the power, but to describe workable methods by which it may be drawn upon and used in connection with the daily problems of men. In the performance of this responsibility, I do not have to rely upon hypotheses, for I have carefully tested and accurately proved formulas on which to depend – formulas which I know to be sound and practical because they have been used successfully by men of outstanding achievements in every walk of life. More than five hundred men of this caliber, who collaborated through a long period of years in the organisation of this philosophy, were specifically questioned on this matter of Controlled Attention, and here is a brief transcript of what some of them said:

Asa Candler, founder of the Coca-Cola business:

"My opinion of the value of concentrated effort can best be stated by mention of the fact that we spend a huge fortune annually for the sole purpose of concentrating the attention of the public on the name 'Coca-Cola'. It may interest you to know that this name is worth many millions of dollars, but it would soon become worthless if we neglected to keep the public's attention concentrated on it."

Henry Ford, founder of the Ford Motor Company:

"My whole life work speaks for itself as to my opinion of the value of concentrated action. Our fortune, our skilled talent, and all our other assets are combined for the sole purpose of giving the public the greatest possible amount of transportation service for the least possible cost. The success of our business has depended, very largely, upon our never having deviated from this policy."

William Wrigley, Jr., the chewing gum 'king':

"What I think about concentrated effort can best be described by examining the five-cent package of chewing gum, to the manufacture and distribution of which I have devoted all my time. Temptations to divert my attention and some of my money into other channels have been many and varied, but I stuck to my original Definite Major Purpose because I recognised, early in life, that no man can succeed if he splits his energies and diverts his attention in many different directions."

(Incidentally, Mr. Wrigley was the first student of my Philosophy of American Achievement, after it had been organised and tested.)

Andrew Carnegie, the man who inspired the organisation of the philosophy, and directed the earlier stages of its organisation had a favorite slogan which he expressed on every appropriate occasion. It was this:

"Place all your eggs in one basket, then watch the basket closely to see that no one kicks it over."

By that he meant, of course, to concentrate all of one's attention upon a single Definite Major Purpose. He did precisely that, in the development of the great steel industry he founded, and in the accumulation of his huge fortune.

King Gillette, producer of the first practical safety razor:

"By concentrating all my attention and my fortune upon the production of a safety razor, I have not only fulfilled a mission in life that has given me great satisfaction and a stable fortune, but I have rendered a priceless service to millions of men who use my product. I have stuck to this one Definite Major Purpose because I realised that an average lifetime is not long enough to permit one to attain more than one major goal."

Edwin C. Barnes, national distributor of the 'Ediphone' and the only business partner that Thomas A. Edison had:

"I have confined my efforts entirely to the sale and distribution of Ediphones [Edison dictating machines] because I learned from Mr. Edison, quite early in life, the benefits of concentrated effort. One of the first of Mr. Edison's traits of character which I observed was his habit of controlling his attention upon one thing at a time. While it is true that he created many different inventions, it must be remembered that he concentrated all of his attention in the field of invention, and always fixed his attention on one invention at a time. To this one habit more than any other, perhaps, does he owe his astounding success as an inventor."

John Wanamaker, the 'merchant king' of Philadelphia: "Controlled Attention, behind a single purpose, is the secret of all human achievement. The man who acquires this art and applies it skillfully thereby connects himself with a source of power that is not available to him through any other method. What this power is, how it can best be tapped and used, are questions beyond my sphere of activity, but I do know that it exists for I have used it as the basis of all my business experience. And I can tell you this about it: It becomes, under certain circumstances, an irresistible power sufficient for the solution of all human problems."

James J. Hill, founder of the Great Northern Railway system: "The man who spreads his energies over many different enterprises resembles the man who shuts his eyes when he aims at an object and fires a gun. He may spread his shot in many different directions without hitting the target. Controlled Attention has been my greatest asset. I have used it during most of the adult period of my life, and particularly in building and operating the Great Northern Railway."

John D. Rockefeller, Sr., founder of the Standard Oil Company:

"From the very first day that I took my first job, as a book-keeper, until this very moment, I have followed the plan of centering my attention upon one thing at a time. Controlled Attention places a man in contact with a source of power that gives him what amounts to a sort of super wisdom in the management of his affairs. I have invested large sums of money in many different businesses and industries, but I earned this money in the business on which I have concentrated most of my thought, the oil business. No part of my attention has been given to any of the industries in which I have made investments, except my own."

Wilbur Wright, co-inventor of the Wright airplane:

"My brother Orville and I always followed the habit of concentrating our attention upon one major purpose, and that was the perfecting of a heavier than air flying machine. If we had split our attention, I doubt that we would ever have built a machine that could have flown successfully."

Frank W. Woolworth, founder of the Woolworth five- and ten-cent stores:

"From the day that I originated the modern Five and Ten Cent Store plan, I have devoted all my attention to my Definite Major Purpose, the operation of our stores. Controlled attention played a much more important part in the success of our business than any other factor. Imitators soon entered the field with plans similar to ours, and some of them did quite well, but we remained steadfast in carrying out our original plan. Perhaps this is why we have been known as the leaders in this field for so many years."

Arthur W. Nash, founder of the Nash made-to-order clothing business:

"Our real success began when we discovered that a business thrives best when everyone connected with it concentrates his mind upon the success of the business. Before we made this discovery, we were working at cross-purposes. By combining Definiteness of Purpose, the Golden Rule Applied, and Controlled Attention, we converted a business that was insolvent into a business that now pays adequate dividends to every person who works in it. The combination of these three principles gave us access to a source of power we had not been using before."

George Pullman, inventor of the modern Pullman sleeping car:

"The change in my economic affairs came when I discovered that a man can do but one thing at a time, if he does it well. My entire time has been concentrated upon the refinement of the Pullman car. This has been responsible, more than anything else, for the success we have enjoyed."

Julius Rosenwald, former owner of Sears, Roebuck & Company:

"Controlled Attention, in combination with Definiteness of Purpose, the Golden Rule Applied, and Creative Vision, have made our company the acknowledged leader in the mail-order merchandising field. Of these latter three principles, I would emphasise the first, because without it, the other two would lose much of their economic significance."

Milo C. Jones, the Wisconsin farmer who made a fortune after being stricken by double paralysis:

"After I lost the use of my body, I concentrated all the powers of my mind on a single idea, the making of Little Pig Sausage, and I was amazed to learn that I could accomplish by Controlled Attention alone much more than I had previously been able to accomplish with the full use of my body. With the aid of the Master Mind principle, I could use the physical capacities of other members of my family, in the management of the business, but the planning that was necessary took place through the concentration of my own mind on that single purpose."

Walter C. Chrysler, the founder of the Chrysler Motor Company:

"I agree with Andrew Carnegie that it is a sound policy for one to place all his eggs in one basket and then watch the basket. The better portion of my life has been devoted to the manufacture and sale of fine motorcars. I have concentrated all my energies on this one Definite Major Purpose. It is surprising what a man can accomplish when he gains the necessary self-discipline to enable him to control his attention by holding it on one thing at a time. Whatever success I have attained has been largely the result of Definiteness of Purpose, the Master Mind principle, Creative Vision, Organised Individual Endeavour, Self-Discipline, and Controlled Attention, with strong emphasis on the latter."

Many readers will remember that tragic year 1933, when Franklin D. Roosevelt became the President for his first term. The business depression had spread fear in the minds of the people, and the whole economic structure was in a state of wild chaos, with banks failing and businesses suspending and men being thrown out of jobs by the tens of thousands. Scare headlines about the 'Business Depression' filled the newspapers, and everyone was talking, thinking, and acting in terms of fear and doubt.

> THOMAS A. Edison became the world's greatest inventor, with practically no schooling, solely by learning to concentrate his full attention on one thing at a time.

Being an experienced student of psychology, the President went to work to stop the stampede of fear. His first move was designed to make use of the principle of Controlled Attention – not on the part of a few, but on the part of all the people of the United States. Let us analyse his action, for here we find many of the principles of this philosophy in operation in a practical way, in one of the greatest emergencies this country has ever known.

The President's first move was to call the leaders of both houses of Congress to the White House for a conference at which he sold them the idea of forgetting party affiliations and concentrating all their efforts on the one task of re-establishing confidence in the minds of the American people.

Then he called in the representatives of the newspapers and engaged them in a similar commitment. The church leaders were asked to engage in the same undertaking, regardless of their denomination, and they complied willingly.

The radio announcers were enlisted in the same cause and they went to work in earnest, selling 'Americanism' to the people of America. The President himself inaugurated his famous 'fireside talks' program and spoke directly to the American people.

In these and other similar endeavours too numerous to mention the people of America were brought together, in one master stroke, utilising application of the principle of Controlled Attention, for the sole purpose of restoring confidence in the American way of life, in the American institutions, and, above all, in the American people themselves. The results were like magic!

Almost overnight the scare headlines about 'Business Depression' were dropped and their places were filled with headlines about 'Business Recovery'. Every adult remembers this circumstance, but one of the great tragedies of it lies in the fact that so few people caught the full significance of the power that brought this rapid change about – the power of Controlled Attention focussed upon a Definite Major Purpose.

An emergency was at hand. In fact, it was a national emergency such as the people had never seen before. Spurred on by the seriousness of this emergency, the people dropped their personal prejudices of race, creed and political leanings, and concentrated their minds upon the one task of restoring confidence, with the result that the whole economic picture began to swing back from failure to success.

Here is an impressive example of what happens when people blend their minds and place their combined mind power back of a Definite Major Purpose, in a spirit of Controlled Attention.

The principle works as well for individuals as it worked for the nation as a whole! There is sufficient power available through any normal brain, if it is organised and directed to a definite end through Controlled Attention, to bring the solution of the individual's major problems of life, not to mention the solution of the minor problems, most of which would not exist if one followed the habit of Controlled Attention in dealing with these problems.

Successful businessmen, and others who have given thought to the subject, have long known that the best way to deal with unpleasant problems is to tackle the hardest of them first, and to do it without fear or procrastination, by centring the attention upon it and keeping it there until a solution has been found. It is surprising to learn how quickly the most embarrassing problems will melt away into nothing when one concentrates his attention upon them with a determined will to liquidate them.

But this is not the way the average person handles such problems. Most people handle unpleasant problems about the same way that the lazy housekeeper keeps house, by sweeping the dirt under the carpet. Little problems grow into big ones when left to run their course, without attention.

As one noted psychologist explained the power of Controlled Attention, "It burns a hole straight through the heart of the knottiest of problems if one places back of it a determined will." And he might well have added that Controlled Attention not only burns a hole through the heart of a problem, but it keeps on until it liquidates what is left around the hole.

The late Cyrus H.K. Curtis, the former owner of the *Saturday Evening Post,* had this to say about the principle of Controlled Attention: "When I first purchased the Saturday Evening Post, it consisted mainly of its name and some debts. My Definite Major Purpose was to make the Post the greatest magazine property in the United States. Back of this aim, I concentrated all my attention, all my money and all my influence with my friends, with a faith in the future of the magazine which had no limitations.

"Because of the lack of operating capital, the first years of the *Post* were fraught with difficulties sufficient to have discouraged anyone with less faith than I had. There were times when I owed more money than I could have raised if I had sold everything I possessed, including the Post, and sometimes my creditors were not generous.

"My closest friends begged me to give up the Post and devote my efforts to something requiring less work and less operating capital; but I had committed myself to do a job and I was determined to do it, no matter how long it required, or what effort had to be put into it.

"I went through many years of this sort of experience, some of them pushing me so far into the red that it looked as if I might never get out. That is, it looked that way to everyone except myself.

"All through those years of hardship I kept my mind concentrated on the job ahead of me, and not on the pleadings of my friends who wished me to give it up and quit. I have always felt a contempt for a quitter, and especially the quitter who gives up before he has made an earnest effort to win.

"Now the big fight is over, and I have won! I have made the *Post* exactly what I started out to make it, a fact to which even my competitors will testify."

"Would I go through the same fight again, if I had it to do over again? Why, yes, of course, I would! There is a sort of compensation that is experienced by the man who has had a stiff fight but has won the battle – a form of compensation which, I fear, others never know."

Whenever you see a copy of the Saturday Evening Post, just say to yourself: Here is physical evidence that Controlled Attention, backed by Definiteness of Purpose, cannot be defeated.

That is about the way the story goes with all men who have attained noteworthy success. All of them go through their 'testing time', as Andrew Carnegie expressed it; that shows what sort of mettle they are made of. I have never heard of any person achieving great success without having gone through difficulties, and unpleasant experiences, and the one quality which best stands out during these periods of 'testing time' is Controlled Attention.

The *Saturday Evening Post* is now one of the great magazines of the country. It is the envy of the magazine publishers' field, but we wonder if the millions of people who read it each week ever take the time to study its early history, or know that it is the product of one man's mind – a man who had vision, and imagination, and enthusiasm, and personal initiative, and the fortitude to carry on when the going was hard. I wonder, too, how many people recognise that the greatness of the *Saturday Evening Post*, as compared with many other magazines that have come and gone since its birth, is measured in almost exact proportion to the difficulties through which Cyrus H.K. Curtis nursed it during its early history.

I have singled out the *Saturday Evening Post* because almost everyone is acquainted with it. The same illustration might well be applied to almost any other great industry, for always there is some one person, or a small group of persons, who concentrate their minds upon a definite purpose and carry a business through its "testing time" before success arrives.

Perhaps there is no greater example in all history of the power of concentrated effort than that which is associated with the history of our own country. The American way of life, as we know it today, was born of struggle and hardship and personal sacrifice that has rarely, if ever, been experienced by those of us who enjoy the privileges of this country.

It would pay every reader to spend a few evenings reading of the early history of the United States – especially that portion of it which began with the Declaration of Independence, when fifty-six brave men signed their names to the most important compact designed to bring freedom to people that the world has ever known.

Today, the people of the United States, as well as the people of most of the other countries of the world, are faced by a world emergency which threatens the destruction of the great American way of life, with all of its blessings and rights of personal liberty and its abundance of opportunities.

As I take inventory of what is happening in this country to destroy the unity of the people, I am puzzled to know why the people do not profit by the experience of those brave men who gave the country its solidity and its security when the country was young and weak. I want, too, to know why the people have so soon forgotten the methods by which the President of the United States stopped the stampede of fear in 1933, and re-established temporary confidence, through the principle of Controlled Attention, backed by a definite purpose.

If these principles were sound in the past, they must be equally as sound today. If unity of the people were helpful a little over 165 years ago, when the nation was being wrested from tyranny, such solidarity should be equally helpful today, in our present crisis. And we might well add that if this principle were helpful to the nation as a whole, it may be equally helpful to any small group who set out to accomplish a desirable end, under the Master Mind principle.

Wherever people coordinate their efforts in a spirit of harmony for the attainment of a definite purpose, and begin to work for its attainment, they find themselves aided by a mysterious power which gives momentum to their efforts. If they happen to be martyrs who have been brought together through persecution, the power available to them is, for some strange reason, apparently increased.

About a hundred years ago, a man by the name of Joseph Smith founded a religion known as 'Mormonism'. A religious war sprang up in the community where Smith and his followers lived, which resulted in the murder of him and his brother Hyrum, while they were confined in a jail in Illinois. The leadership of the group was taken over by Brigham Young, who moved a majority of them into the then wilderness of Utah, two thousand miles from the more populous section of the United States. They carried with them barely enough food and seed for planting and utensils for household and farming purposes to keep them from starving to death. After cutting their way through two thousand miles of wilderness, fighting Indians and battling against the elements, they finally arrived at what is now Salt Lake City, Utah, and settled. They planted what seed they carried with them, but it had no sooner sprouted above the ground than it was set upon by grasshoppers and almost devoured.

To add to their miseries, the United States government sent soldiers to Utah, ostensibly to put down polygamy. They went at the job so crudely that they antagonised the entire Mormon population, but the Mormons held out and the little colony survived.

The stories told by the Mormons, of their sacrifices, were almost unbelievable, but they have been substantiated in all of the essential details. The years went by and the Mormons grew and prospered, making their living entirely from the soil.

It is generally conceded that no group of people, throughout the pioneering days of this country, from the early pilgrim settlers on down to the present, were harassed and persecuted as severely as were the Mormons.

Today, a little less than a hundred years after the Mormons settled in Utah, we find them peaceful and prosperous people, still making their living, for the most part, from the soil of the earth. During the Depression, while millions of people were on government relief throughout the nation, the Mormons were the first to announce that thereafter no Mormon would ask for charity. They had found a way to become self-sustaining and determining.

Now, we are not interested in the Mormon religion as such, nor are we interested in the Mormon people except to call attention to what happens when a group of people is driven to martyrdom, as the Mormons were. Here we have a convincing example of the soundness of Andrew Carnegie's motto that "adversity carries with it the seed of an equivalent benefit".

The Mormons met with adversity on a scale almost beyond human endurance. As to the merits or demerits of their cause, or their religion, or their former domestic relationships, we are in no way interested; but we are keenly interested in learning the secret by which a group of people may so combine their fortunes and their efforts that each individual may get the necessities of life without asking for public charity.

Study the Mormons carefully and you will find that the 'secret' of their self-determination, if there is anything about it that can be called secret, dates back to the spirit of perseverance which they developed while fighting for their lives. They were driven to pool their scant economic resources and their spiritual resources for their defense against a society that was trying to exterminate them.

In forming that pool, they discovered something which should be of keen interest to the rest of us. They discovered that there is power in unity of purpose and coordination of physical effort. They not only discovered the Master Mind principle, but they used it to save themselves from total annihilation and used it to save themselves from the humility of accepting public charity, in an era when millions of other people who were never persecuted were seeking subsidy through government relief.

The Mormons not only understand the principle of Controlled Attention, but that principle has been used by them so successfully that they have wrested victory from defeat, in a world that was bent upon destroying them. Their application of this principle was, at first, a matter of necessity. They were forced to concentrate their attention upon a Definite Major Purpose or be annihilated. Later, perhaps, they began making use of the principle out of preference, because they had learned of its stupendous power while fighting for existence.

Before leaving the subject of the Mormons I wish to make one other observation concerning them. Today, they have missionaries in practically every part of the United States, and in most of the countries of the world. Having made a place for themselves under the most severe conditions, they are now being recognised throughout the world, as favourably as they were once persecuted.

There is no spirit of revenge among the Mormon people today. If they ever felt revengeful for the persecution they were forced to undergo, it has now been subdued. They hold no grudges against anyone on any score. Perhaps that may be one reason why they are being accepted so freely throughout the world. Their 'Mental attitude' is positive and constructive. They are loyal American citizens, conforming in every way to the best and most approved habits of the American way of life.

In all this country, no finer example of the soundness of Emerson's essay on compensation can be found than that of the Mormons. That which was taken from them by the generation of a hundred years ago is now being freely and willingly repaid to them by this generation. Here is food for thought of the highest order!

Let us recognise truth wherever we find it. Moreover, let us appropriate truth and make use of it, no matter from what source it may come. If the Mormons have a better way of relating themselves to one another than have the rest of us, let us discover their way and make use of it. Let us be fair – to our

-selves at least – and analyse the Mormon way of life, not by their habits of a hundred years ago, but their habits of today!

The whole world is in a state of maladjustment. Human relationships have been disturbed in this and all other countries, to a point of danger which threatens civilisation. It behooves us, therefore, to observe the methods of any individual or group of individuals who have found a way to relate themselves to life harmoniously.

When we find even one person who has discovered how to live harmoniously with the rest of the world, let us inquire into his philosophy, for despite the fact we may come into his presence to scoff, we may find it advantageous to remain and pray!

Controlled Attention makes this sort of analysis possible. It enables one to pierce the outer covering of things and people as they appear to be, and to learn what exists under the covering! The world needs this sort of analysis right now. Most of us are too much inclined to view the outward appearances and the material aspects of things and people, overlooking the reality that lies underneath. And this tragic habit has brought the whole world to the very brink of spiritual bankruptcy.

This philosophy was intended, originally, as a philosophy of individual achievement, designed mainly to enable people to procure the material needs of life without violating the rights of others. Mr. Carnegie had this in mind when he inspired the research which resulted in the philosophy. But the changed conditions of the world, since Mr. Carnegie's time, have led me to look at an entirely new world; a world of spiritual wealth; a world in which the finer arts of human relationship have been revealed; and it is the greater spirit of understanding that I wish the reader of this chapter to acquire.

I have endeavoured to show that there is a difference between Controlled Attention and ordinary concentration of efforts. Let us make sure that we understand the nature and extent of this difference. The word 'control' is the key to the explanation of the difference. Controlled Attention means the act of coordinating all the faculties of the mind and directing their combined power to a given end! Such is an act which requires self-discipline of the highest order. It also requires the development of controlled habits. As a matter of fact, one cannot control attention without the supporting influence of well-developed habits of thought.

Now let us consider some of the circumstances under which Controlled Attention is applied, viz.:

(a) Prayer: When one prays, if he understands the true meaning of prayer, and prays in a state of mind that has been cleared of all fear and doubt, he does so by setting aside his own faculty of reason, his faculty of will, and all other faculties of the mind except the faculty of the emotions. With the mind under control, he concentrates all his positive emotions, especially the emotion of faith, on the object of his prayer, having such a deep faith in its attainment that he can see himself already in possession of it. Under this sort of Controlled Attention, one makes direct connection with Infinite Intelligence. If the prayer is answered favourably, the answer comes in the form of an inspired idea, plan, or method by which one may, through his own efforts, acquire that for which he prays.

The words used in prayer are immaterial. The state of mind in which the prayer is offered is the thing that counts! The factor of faith must be present. The slightest shade of fear or doubt or indecision in connection with one's right to get that for which he prays will bring negative results. The mind must be free from every other thought except that connected with the object of the prayer. The prayer must continue until it produces the desired results. Sometimes this happens within a matter of seconds; at other times the answer may be deferred for hours, days, months, or years, according to the nature of the prayer and what is necessary for its fulfillment.

Prayer expressed in times of emergency, when the mind is dominated by fear, has seldom been known to produce the desired results, although the one who prays may be in great need of aid.

Prayer based on a request for something which would call for the cessation of natural law, or the circumvention or violation of natural law, will bring negative results.

Prayer asking for results that would damn others fails, also, and for the very understandable reason that the person who makes such a request has in his mind some form of revenge, greed, selfishness, or other negative emotion which renders the prayer ineffective.

Successful prayer depends upon adequate preparation of the mind for the expression of prayer. That preparation is Controlled Attention based on faith!

Prayer is Power

Dr. Alexis Carrel, who devoted thirty-three years to biological research at the Rockefeller Institute, and is the author of Man, the Unknown, analysed prayer as follows:

"Prayer is not only worship; it is also an invisible emanation of man's worshipping spirit – the most powerful form of energy that one can generate. The influence of prayer on the human mind and body is as demonstrable as that of secreting glands. Its results can be measured in terms of increased physical buoyancy, greater intellectual vigour, moral stamina, and a deeper understanding of the realities underlying human relationships.

"If you make a habit of sincere prayer, your life will be very noticeably and profoundly altered. Prayer stamps with its indelible mark our actions and demeanour. A tranquility of bearing, a facial and bodily repose are observed in those whose inner lives are thus enriched. Within the depths of consciousness, a flame kindles. And man sees himself. He discovers himself. He discovers his selfishness, his silly pride, his fears, his greed, his blunders. He develops a sense of moral obligation, intellectual humility. Thus begins a journey of the soul towards the realm of grace.

"Prayer is a force as real as terrestrial gravity. As a physician, I have seen men, after all other therapy had failed, lifted out of disease and melancholy by the serene effort of prayer. It is the only power in the world that seems to overcome the so-called 'laws of nature'; the occasions on which prayer has dramatically done this have been termed 'miracles'! But a constant, quieter miracle takes place hourly in the hearts of men and women who have discovered that prayer supples them with a steady flow of sustaining power in their daily lives.

"Too many people regard prayer as a formalised routine of words, a refuge for weaklings, or a childish petition for material things. We sadly undervalue prayer when we conceive it in these terms, just as we should underestimate rain by describing it as something that fills the birdbath in our garden. Properly understood, prayer is a mature activity indispensable to the fullest development of personality – the ultimate integration of man's highest faculties. Only in prayer do we achieve that complete and harmonious assembly of body, mind and spirit which gives the frail human reed its unshakable strength.

"The words 'Ask and it shall be given to you' have been verified by the experience of humanity. True, prayer may not restore the dead child to life or bring relief from physical pain. But prayer, like radium, is a source of luminous, self-generating energy.

"How does prayer fortify us with so much dynamic power? To answer this question (admittedly outside the jurisdiction of science), I must point out that all prayers have one thing in common. The triumphant hosannas of a great oratorio, or the humble supplication of an Iroquois hunter begging for luck in the chase, demonstrate the same truth: that human beings seek to augment their finite energy by addressing themselves to the Infinite source of all energy. When we pray, we link ourselves with the inexhaustible motive power that spins the universe. We ask that a part of this power be apportioned to our needs. Even in asking, our human deficiencies are minimised and we arise strengthened and repaired.

"But we must never summon God merely for the gratification of our whims. We derive most power from prayer when we use it not as a petition but as a supplication that we may become more like Him. Prayer should be regarded as practice of the Presence of God. An old peasant was seated alone in the last pew of the village church. 'What are you waiting for?' he was asked; and he answered, 'I am looking at Him and He is looking at me.' Man prays not only that God should remember him, but also that he should remember God.

"How can prayer be defined? Prayer is the effort of man to reach God, to commune with an invisible being, creator of all things, supreme wisdom, truth, beauty, and strength, father and redeemer of each man. This goal of prayer always remains hidden to intelligence. For both language and thought fail when we attempt to describe God.

"We do know, however, that whenever we address God in fervent prayer, we change both soul and body for the better. It could not happen that any man or woman could pray for a single moment without some good result. 'No man ever prayed,' said Emerson, 'without learning something'.

"One can pray everywhere. In the streets, the subway, the office, the shop, the school, as well as in the solitude of one's own room or among the crowd in a church. There is no prescribed posture, time or place."

"'Think of God more often than you breathe,' said Epictetus, the Stoic. In order really to mold personality, prayer must become a habit. It is meaningless to pray in the morning and to live like a barbarian the remainder of the day. True prayer is a way of life; the truest life is literally a way of prayer.

"The best prayers are like the improvisations of gifted lovers, always about the same thing yet never twice the same. We cannot all be as creative in prayer as Saint Teresa or Bernard of Clairvaux, both of whom poured their adoration into words of mystical beauty. Fortunately, we do not need their eloquence; our slightest impulse to prayer is recognised by God. Even if we are pitifully dumb, or if our tongues are overlaid with vanity or deceit, our meager syllables of praise are acceptable to him, and he showers us with strengthening manifestations of his love.

"Today, as never before, prayer is a binding necessity in the lives of men and nations. The lack of emphasis on the religious sense has brought the world to the edge of destruction. Our deepest source of power and perfection has been left miserably undeveloped. Prayer, the basic exercise of the spirit, must be actively practiced in our private lives. The neglected soul of man must be made strong enough to assert itself once more. For if the power of prayer is again released and used in the lives of common men and women; if the spirit declares its aims clearly and boldly, there is yet hope that our prayers for a better world will be answered."

Quoted by permission from the Reader's Digest.

(b) Definiteness of Purpose. Here one must understand the full significance of Andrew Carnegie's emphasis on the relationship of perfect harmony between all the minds of a Master Mind group. Lack of harmony on the part of one individual of the group will destroy the Controlled Attention feature of the alliance. It is obvious, therefore, that Controlled Attention is more easily attained by an individual than it is by a group of individuals, because of the difficulty in bringing together a group of people all of whom will subordinate their personal desires and motives for the attainment of a common end.

The Mormon people accomplished this end, but they were inspired to do so by one of the strongest of all motives, the desire for self-preservation. It is very easy for one to subordinate his personal desires for the good of his associates when his very life depends upon mutual coordination of effort, in spirit as well as in deed.

Mr. Carnegie has called attention, time and again, to the necessity of perfect harmony in a Master Mind alliance. His genius in maintaining that relationship between the members of his Master Mind group and himself was the major secret of his stupendous achievements. He so arranged his relationship with his Master Mind allies that all of them became wealthy far beyond anything they might have accomplished working independently, without his aid. Being the astute judge of human nature that he was, he recognised that men control their attention because of adequate motive, and for no other reason. He provided his Master Mind allies with many motives for cooperating with him in a spirit of perfect harmony, not the least of these being the desire for financial gain.

Sales managers who understand practical psychology often inspire their salesmen to exert extra effort by holding out to them extra compensation in the form of bonuses, prizes, personal privileges, etc. The more successful sales managers usually manage to have some sort of a system of extra compensation in operation all of the time, because experience has proved that this is the best known method of inducing men to take possession of their own minds and work towards a common end in a spirit of harmony.

The sales manager of less experience often resorts to other methods for sales production results, such as holding his salesmen in fear of the loss of their jobs. Such methods sometimes produce temporary results that seem to be satisfactory, but they are only temporary. Permanent success in any sort of human relationship must be founded on mutual confidence and the spirit of harmony. Human relationships based on any other foundation are destined to fail, no matter what may be the nature of the relationship, or for what purpose it is formed! Let us all remember this, with profit.

The world is now passing through an emergency when most of the people seem to have overlooked the importance of harmonious human relationships! There can be no harmony of human relationships in a world that is dominated by selfishness, greed, envy, revenge, hatred, lust, avarice, fear, doubt, indecision, and the desire for something for nothing which are so evident throughout the world today.

There can be no peace of mind or permanent success for the individual who is dominated by any of these negative states of mind. Controlled Attention is one of the major principles by which all negative states of mind may be eliminated.

In a recent radio address Pope Pius expressed the opinion that the world war is God's way of purging a sin-sick world of its sins. Common sense suggests that the people of the world (with exceptions, of course) have been relating themselves to one another, since the beginning of the First World War, in a manner deserving of correction.

(c) Love: Here is a state of mind, a human emotion, which heads the entire list of all emotions for effectiveness in establishing harmonious relationships between people. Love is of the spirit; it is of Divine origin. If you wish to see Controlled Attention in operation in its highest form, observe the man and woman who have consolidated their interests in a spirit of love. Observe, also, how easily this state of mind clears the mind of all other thoughts. Where true love prevails, the presence of envy, greed, revenge, lust, selfishness, and the desire for something for nothing claim no part of the minds of the lovers.

I am not referring to that form of sentimentalism known as 'puppy love', nor the emotion of sex which is often mistaken for love. I am speaking of that spiritual power which brings people together in a spirit of oneness; that relationship through which each person becomes (spiritually) a part of the other!

Love is spiritual harmony between two people. The relationship is not confined to men and women. It is the sort of relationship that exists between people wherever the true spirit of Christianity prevails. It has nothing in common with dogma or creed. It is the highest form of human intercourse. Where it becomes the dominating factor in human relationships, harmony and understanding exist. It is Controlled Attention directed to a Definiteness of Purpose among people. He whom it affects recognises, willingly, that he is 'his brother's keeper'.

It was this Divine spirit of love which inspired the signers of the Declaration of Independence voluntarily and willingly to pawn their own lives in order that liberty might be the common privilege of their fellow men. Their motive had nothing of the nature of selfishness in it. It had no relationship to fear. It was the product of an enduring faith that was shared alike by fifty-six men who were so sure of the justice of their cause that they saw it triumphant, at the outset. Wherever men *control their attention* and direct it to a definite end, in this spirit, they avail themselves of a source of power which may successfully defy opposition. That sort of power never is used by despots, for it is an impossibility to use spiritual power destructively. Spiritual power builds, but never tears down.

Controlled Attention leads to mastery in any sort of endeavour, because it enables one to focus the powers of his mind upon a definite objective and keep it so directed, at will. Controlled Attention is self-mastery of the highest order, for it is an accepted fact that the man who can control his own mind can control everything that gets in his way.

The man who knows exactly what he wants, and who concentrates his attention upon getting it with the full backing of his will to win, usually is not disappointed. Nothing can defeat him except a stronger opposing will. That sort of concentrated effort finds a way to master obstacles which seem insurmountable. It was this sort of willpower that Harriet Beecher Stowe had in mind when she wrote:

"When you get into a tight place and everything goes against you, until it seems as though you could not hold on a minute longer, never give up then for that is just the place and time that the tide will turn."

Yes, the tide seems always to turn in one's favour if one is determined to see that it does. The state of mind has a lot to do with the 'tide'. Plato had in mind this same thought when he said:

"The first and best victory is to conquer self; to be conquered by self is, of all things, the most shameful and vile."

Every great philosopher who has given thought to the powers of the mind has discovered that the mind has within it qualities sufficient for every emergency. Henry Wadsworth Longfellow recognised the truth of this when he said:

"An enlightened mind is not hoodwinked; it is not shut up in a gloomy prison till it thinks the walls of its own dungeon are the limits of the universe, and the reach of its own chain the outer verge of intelligence."

While Longfellow did not try to explain the source of the mind's power, he definitely recognised the irresistible power of the mind, just as every deep thinker recognises it.

Parkman showed his understanding of the mind and particularly the power of a concentrated mind when he wrote:

"He who would do some great thing in this short life must apply himself to work with such concentration of his forces as, to idle spectators, who live only to amuse themselves, looks like insanity."

And Annie Besant expressed her deep and mature understanding of the power that is available through the mind when she said:

"Knowledge is essential to conquest; only according to our ignorance are we helpless. Thought creates character. Character can dominate conditions. Will creates circumstances and environment."

Thomas Fowell Buxton expressed a great truth in connection with the power of concentrated thought when he wrote:

"The longer I live, the more deeply I am convinced that which makes the difference between one man and another – between the weak and the weak and the powerful, the great and the insignificant – is energy, invincible determination, a purpose once formed and then death or victory."

Every man who has triumphed over prolonged defeat will understand the meaning of Buxton's statement.

Arnold Bennett expressed his understanding of mind power when he said:

"The manner in which one single ray of light, one single precious hint, will clarify and energise the whole mental life of him who receives it, is among the most wonderful and heavenly of intellectual phenomena.... I think it rather fine, this necessity for the tense bracing of the will before anything worth doing can be done. I feel it is the chief thing that differentiates men from the cat by the fire."

Whenever one tunes in on the thoughts of men who really think, he discovers evidence of their recognition of the irresistible power of the mind when that power is organised and turned to a definite purpose.

MAN IS not a creature of circumstances, but a creator of circumstances. He makes his own circumstances, his own opportunities.

John Quincy Adams expressed his belief in the profound nature of the power of the mind in these words: *"Courage and perseverance have a magic talisman before which difficulties disappear and obstacles vanish into air."*

Washington Irving expressed his respect for the powers of the mind when he said:

"Great minds have purposes, others have wishes. Little minds are tamed and subdued by misfortune; but great minds rise above them."

Yes, that is true; great minds do rise above misfortunes, and let us not forget that one of the qualities which make a great mind is that of definiteness of purpose backed by concentration of effort. John Foster expressed a great truth concerning the influence of a positive mind that is backed by determination, when he said:

"When a firm, decisive spirit is recognised, it is curious to see how the space clears around a man and leaves him room and freedom."

I have observed the truth of this, many times, by watching a determined man who knew where he was going, as he walked down the street. I have actually seen people look back over their shoulders, become confused, and quickly sidestep out of his way. The determined mind projects an influence that is felt by everyone within its range. You can recognise that sort of mind the moment one who possesses it walks into a room that is crowded by people, even though you may not actually see the man. His presence makes itself felt!

Ralph Waldo Emerson disclosed his profound understanding of the power of thought in these words:

"The key to every man is his thought.... Beware when the great God lets loose a thinker on this planet."

I take you, now, to Mr. Carnegie's analysis of this concept, but I wish to remind you that the method by which the habit of Controlled Attention can best be developed has been described in the first portion of this chapter. Mr. Carnegie's analysis will deal mainly with the effects of controlled attention, rather than the method by which this desirable habit may be acquired.

□

Andrew Carnegie's Analysis of Controlled Attention

The analysis begins in Mr. Carnegie's private study in 1908 when I first met and interviewed him.

HILL:

Mr. Carnegie, will you describe how Controlled Attention can be applied in the practical affairs of life?

CARNEGIE:

Now let us define the term 'Controlled Attention', and make sure we understand exactly what it means. It is the act of combining all the faculties of the mind and concentrating them upon the attainment of a definite purpose. The time involved in the act of concentration of thought on a given subject depends upon the nature of the subject and upon that which one expects in connection with it. Take my own case, for example. The dominating forces of my mind are, and have been for many years, concentrated upon the making and the marketing of steel. I have others allied with me who likewise concentrate their dominating thoughts upon the same objective. Thus, we have the benefit of Controlled Attention in collective form, consisting, as it does, of the individual mind power of a great number of people, all working towards the same end, in a spirit of harmony.

HILL:

Could you not have carried on other business activities just as successfully as you conducted the steel industry, and at the same time? Wouldn't the Master Mind principle have made this possible?

CARNEGIE:

Yes, I have known men to conduct many separate, unrelated businesses successfully, with the aid of the Master Mind; but I have always believed they would have done much better had they confined their efforts entirely to one line of business. Splitting one's attention has the effect of dividing one's powers. The best plan for anyone to follow is to devote all his energies to some specific field. This concentration enables one to specialise in that field.

HILL:

But, what about the doctors who engage in general practice? Do they not have a better opportunity to add to their income than those who specialise in one particular branch of medicine?

CARNEGIE:

No, the exact opposite is true. If you ever have occasion to engage a specialist to remove your appendix, as I have had, you will learn that specialisation in medicine pays. When I was a small boy, the old family physician who used to look after the health of the people of our neighbourhood would have removed an appendix for $25, and I suspect he could have done the job about as well as the specialist who charged me more than ten times that amount. But, I called in the specialist just the same.

HILL:

Does this same rule apply in the field of retail merchandising?

CARNEGIE:

Yes, it applies in every line of business and every calling. Modern merchandising has practically made the old-fashioned general store obsolete. While the most prosperous stores are departmentalised, they are not the same as the old general merchandise stores, because each department is managed by a specialist who devotes all his time to that department. You might say that a modern department store is nothing but a group of highly specialised stores, all operating under one roof and one general overhead, but possessing increased buying power that gives the store a tremendous advantage over smaller stores.

HILL: You would say, then, that the department store is managed under the principle of Controlled Attention?

CARNEGIE:

That and other principles of the philosophy of individual achievement, especially the Master Mind principle and Definiteness of Purpose.

HILL:

What about the banking business? Is it managed, also, by application of the principle of Controlled Attention?

CARNEGIE:

Very much so! Every department of a large bank, and practically every individual position in each department, is highly specialised. The same is true of railroading. Practically every position in the railroad business is specialised. Promotions are from the bottom upward, and the men holding the more responsible positions have had training in nearly all the subordinate positions, but they never undertake to hold two jobs at the same time. It is the same in the steel industry. Men become highly skilled by confining their efforts to specialised work. Here, too, promotions are from the bottom upward. All of our headmen have served their apprenticeship in subordinate jobs in the operating end of the business.

HILL:

You believe, then, that the better opportunities of the future will be available to those who concentrate their efforts along some specialised lines?

CARNEGIE:

It has always been that way and it always will be.

HILL:

What about the profession of teaching? Is it not possible for a teacher to prepare himself to teach many different subjects?

CARNEGIE:

Oh, yes, it is possible, but not advisable. The big universities are nothing but a group of associated colleges, each specialising in some particular branch of education. If it were practical for a teacher to do better work by devoting his efforts to a diversity of subjects, the universities would have discovered this long ago.

HILL:

What about the student who is preparing himself for

a life work? Should he specialise in some particular branch of education?

CARNEGIE:

Yes, if he knows what his Definite Major Purpose in life is to be. Otherwise he should confine his efforts to a general educational course until such time as he chooses a goal. Then he should continue his education through specialised training. The lawyer, for example, usually takes a course in general education, and then specialises in law. The doctor usually does likewise. General education gives one an approach to organised thinking, self-discipline, and self-reliance – all essential qualities for success in any calling.

HILL:

What about the stenographer? Should he or she concentrate on one line of work?

CARNEGIE:

Well, the stenographer must specialise, obviously, before procuring a position. After that he may have to engage in general service for a time, but the stenographer who does not wish to remain in that sort of work takes stock of his opportunities while engaged in general office work, and sooner or later specialised in some particular department through which he can promote himself to a better position. Many of the more successful business and industrial leaders of out times got their start through stenographic positions, where they had an opportunity to study the methods of their superiors. This is among the finest of all types of office work as far as preparation for executive responsibilities is concerned. The stenographer literally goes to a school taught by highly skilled executives and is paid for doing so.

HILL:

What about the farmer? Should he specialise also?

CARNEGIE:

Yes, he should, but usually he does not. This is one of the major weaknesses of agriculture. The men who are making the most money from the soil are those who specialise in certain crops, such as wheat, rye, barley and corn. The farmer who raises a little of everything very seldom receives much for anything he raises.

HILL:

What about the book-keeper? Should he specialise too?

CARNEGIE:

Yes, unless he is contented to remain always a book-keeper, and even then he will make more from his work if he specialises in a particular branch of accounting. The better-paid men in this field usually branch out from general book-keeping to auditing and the installation of accounting systems. A clever man in this field finds it quite profitable, for every business beyond the one-man size needs dependable records of its transactions. The jack-of-all-trades usually is good at none!

There is some part that everyone can take in the scheme of affairs – some part through which he can render useful service and gain his just compensation. It is everyone's responsibility to find out what this part is, and to prepare himself for it. All well-ordered life requires preparation. Before one begins to prepare, he should know for what he is preparing himself. That, within itself, is concentration of effort. The man who has no definite purpose in life, who cannot do some one thing and do it well, is like a dry leaf on the bosom of the wind. He will be tossed here and there, wherever the winds of chance carry him, but, like the rolling stone, he will gather no moss. Unfortunately, the majority of people spend their lives in thus rolling!

HILL:

Do you mean that a man should choose his Definite Major Purpose before beginning his education, and prepare himself to specialise in connection with that aim?

CARNEGIE:

No, not always. Seldom is a very youthful person, who has not finished his basic education, in a position to adopt a Definite Major Purpose. In that case he should complete his essential education, through the grades and high school. If he still is unable to choose a major purpose in life he should either go to work and learn, from experience, of the possibilities of different occupations, or go to college and take a general liberal arts educational course. After that, one should be able to decide what calling he wishes to follow.

HILL:

Suppose a person chooses a Definite Major Purpose, but finds, after he pursues it for a while, that he dislikes it, or he finds something he likes better? Should he make a change?

CARNEGIE:

Yes, by all means! A man will succeed best in that which he likes best, all else being equal. It is advisable for one to change, provided he does not get into the habit of changing every time the work he has chosen becomes difficult, or he meets with temporary defeat. Changing from one line of work to another involves a tremendous loss. It is something like an industrial plant, the management of which changes from one product to another. The successful person must reach the stage of specialisation, sooner or later; the sooner, the better.

HILL:

Is it advisable for a businessman to engage in politics?

CARNEGIE:

Not if he wishes to succeed in business. Politics is a profession unto itself, and not a very dependable one at that. But it is a profession, and those who succeed best at it are those who do nothing else.

HILL:

What sort of career would you advise a young man to choose? A professional career or a business career?

CARNEGIE:

That depends upon the young man, his likes and dislikes, his native ability, his physical conditions, etc. Generally speaking, I would say that business and industry offer much broader opportunities than do the professions, because the professions are overcrowded already. This is essentially an industrial nation. Industry is the backbone of our economic structure. And I have never seen the time when a reliable, loyal, and capable man could not find his place in industry. Here is where most of the larger fortunes are made, which, within itself, partly answers your question, since most people choose a career with the object of earning a living and accumulating as much wealth as possible. There always has been a shortage of capable men at the head of industry, but never a shortage in the professions.

HILL:

What about the army, or the navy, or the government service as a career? Are there desirable opportunities in any of these three branches of service?

CARNEGIE:

Again I must say that this depends very largely on the person who is choosing the career. If a man wishes an opportunity to engage in a creative effort, he would not choose the government service as career, since his chances there would become a matter of the whims of politicians. He would fare better in either the army or the navy, since these are somewhat further removed from political influence. Some have made commendable records in both of these fields of the service, but generally they were men who liked that sort of life.

The line of promotion in both the army and the navy is rather long and by no means easy. Military service calls for concentrated effort and a definite limitation of ambition, as the possibilities of advancement are known in advance. Some men are not suited, by nature, to limit themselves in this manner. They prefer to take their chances in business or industry, where the risks may be greater and the work harder, but the possibilities of achievement are without any fixed limits.

HILL:

Then you recommend concentration of effort, through specialisation, in all calling? You believe, obviously, in a "one-track" mind?

CARNEGIE:

Specialisation, through concentration of effort, gives one greater power. It saves lost motion in both thought and physical action. It harmonises with the principle of Definiteness of Purpose, the starting point of all achievement. I believe in a one-track mind if you allow me to describe it this way: a wide range of knowledge based on facts related to one's major purpose, but expressed through organised plans for the attainment of that purpose. I might make my meaning better understood if I stated it this way: A man should have a multiple-track mind for the accumulation of knowledge, but a single-track mind for the expression of that knowledge, which is about the same as saying that one should have a reserve of both general and specific knowledge, but he should concentrate its use upon the attainment of a Definite Major Purpose.

> YOU MAY have everything you desire if you desire it badly enough to inspire you to keep your mind fixed on its attainment.

Knowledge gives one no power until it is organised and expressed in action! That requires concentration of effort. A man may be a walking encyclopedia of general knowledge, and I have known such people – but his knowledge will be practically useless until he organises it and gives it some form of expression, through definiteness of purpose.

Now, if you wish an excellent example of the power of Controlled Attention I'll give you one. You are a young man, with most of your life ahead of you. Sooner or later, no doubt, you will give some thought to marriage, but before you make a choice you may look around considerably, analysing many 'suspects,' before you find an acceptable 'prospect' for marriage. When you find one whom you believe to be your choice, observe how quickly and definitely you will begin to concentrate your attention upon this one woman! There's the time and the place to watch your step, for concentration of effort leads to climax of action, and this applies not only in the choice of a mate in marriage, but in all other human relationships. Concentration of attention leads to lasting friendships, and permanent business alliances, and to other permanent relationships. It leads to repeated successes, and over time 'success consciousness' becomes a habit.

HILL:

You speak of 'success consciousness' as becoming a habit. I have observed that most people have a 'failure consciousness'. How is this habit acquired?

CARNEGIE:

By the same method that the 'success consciousness' is acquired, the concentration of attention upon failure and habits that lead to failure. Such habits, for example, as procrastination, fear, indecision, and indifference to opportunity. Through the principle of autosuggestion, one's dominating thoughts and physical habits become a fixed part of one's permanent character. Concentration of thought on any subject attracts to one the circumstances by which the physical counterpart of the thought is created.

HILL:

And it is by this means that thought becomes transformed into physical things?

CARNEGIE:

I would state it slightly differently. It is by this means that thought attracts one to its physical counterpart. Thought does not actually become transformed into material things; or at least we have no substantial evidence that it does; but thought does attract some combination of circumstances by which its physical counterpart is assembled or drawn to one. And it does this by the aid of whatever natural means are available. For example, Definiteness of Purpose inspires one to engage in physical action in carrying out the object of that purpose. Thus, while thought did not actually attract the physical counterpart of the purpose, it inspired the individual to procure it, through the most logical means available.

HILL:

Then there is no mystery connected with your statement that one's dominating thoughts tend to clothe themselves in their physical counterpart?

CARNEGIE:

None whatsoever. The method by which this takes place is as understandable as the multiplication table or the rules of grammar.

HILL:

But there are schools of thought whose followers would have one believe that one's dominating thoughts, such as one engages in when praying, can attract their physical counterpart through some inexplicable mystery, or supernatural law.

CARNEGIE:

Well, they could be right about this, but I have never knowingly acquired any desirable results from thought, through any means that I could not explain by the laws of nature and the rules of ordinary human relationship. I have never depended upon supernatural law, for truthfully I know of no such law.

I will say this, however: The circumstances through which Definiteness of Purpose attracts opportunities favourable to the realisation of the purpose often are so unexpected that they appear inexplicable. I suspect, however, that accurate analysis would disclose that there is a perfectly logical and purely natural cause for every effect! Sometimes the effects of certain experiences of our lives are so far removed from the actual cause that we completely lose sight of the cause.

I will give you a splendid example of what I mean: Some years ago, I called in a young man who had been serving as the secretary to one of our executives, and, with very little explanation, promoted him to a very responsible executive position, at a big increase in salary. He was so surprised that he told one of his friends that the promotion was a 'miracle'.

Well, it may have seemed like a miracle to him, but let me tell you what caused it! That young man had acquired certain desirable habits which made him more valuable in a higher position. For example, he arrived at his work a half hour earlier than the rules of his department required, and did not quit work for an hour or more after the others in his department had gone home for the day. On many occasions, he came back at night, when there was extra work to be done. No one asked him to do this. He was not given extra pay for doing it. But, he moved entirely on his own initiative, thus advertising to the management that he possessed initiative of a high order. Now, remember that personal initiative is a rare quality, and it is one of the major essentials of those who assume the responsibility of leadership in any calling. Well, the habit of Going the Extra Mile was the first quality that attracted our attention to this young man.

After he had come to our attention in this favourable light, we also observed that he had the habit of doing his work more neatly and thoroughly than others who were engaged in similar work.

Then we noticed that he had an abundance of enthusiasm through which he inspired those around him to work in the right sort of mental attitude. We sent out an investigator and discovered that he was taking a night course in engineering, thus proving that he had definiteness of purpose. The investigator discovered, also, that this young man's home life was pleasant and he was popular with the neighbours, thus proving that he had an attractive personality.

Now, in view of these discoveries, do you see anything in connection with his promotion that savoured of the supernatural, or the miraculous? Yet, these are the sort of 'miracles' which enable some to get ahead while others around them, who have just as much education and as much knowledge of their work, fail to get ahead.

We promoted this young man because, by his own habits, his own mental attitude and self-discipline, he had earned the right to promotion. When the promotion came, it came as the result of the natural cause of promotions. Perhaps the promotion seemed like a 'miracle' to him because it came before he had planned it. And that is another queer thing about men who prepare themselves for the better things of life. The better things have a way of appearing before they are expected.

HILL:

And you believe that it is through similar circumstances that all men who succeed attain their success?

CARNEGIE:

I am sure of it! I have had the privilege of promoting as many men as has any other industrialist in America, if not, in fact, more. I have carefully analysed the cause of every promotion I have made and I can state definitely that every such promotion was earned well in advance by the person who was promoted. The only part I took in the transaction was to discover those who had earned promotions, and generally speaking I did not have to spend much time in this direction, because men who prepare themselves for promotion develop habits which are so obvious that they cannot be overlooked by an intelligent employer who, if he succeeds, must be eternally on the lookout for men who are capable of assuming responsibilities.

You may think that a promotion is a great favour to the one promoted, but let me tell you that it is no greater favour to him than it is to the man who does the promoting, provided he picks the man who is entitled to promotion. But, in final analysis, all just promotions are self-acquired, through self-discipline, training and preparation.

HILL:

You do not believe, then, that chance or luck favours one under such circumstances?

CARNEGIE:

Only to this extent: It sometimes happens that the time of a man's promotion is the result of some form of luck or chance, such as the death of a person to whose position he is promoted, or an emergency calling for some special form of talent which the promoted person possesses, but the 'luck' is related only to the time. Such a person who is entitled to promotion will get it sooner or later, luck or no luck, because every man gravitates to the place in life where he belongs, by preparation and acquired habit, as naturally as water flows downhill. Nothing can change this, no matter by what name one calls the circumstance. He can call it luck, or a fortunate break, or whatever he pleases; but let me tell you that the only sort of luck any man can depend upon is that which he provides for himself, through painstaking preparation for whatever he desires in life.

HILL:

Your analysis indicates that Controlled Attention is an important feature in one's preparation for promotion, or the attainment of any definite purpose.

CARNEGIE:

Yes, an indispensable feature, you might say. It is impossible for a man to develop the habit of self-discipline – so necessary as a means of preparation for the attainment of a definite purpose –

without concentration of his attention. He should practise this art until it becomes a habit. The place to begin is with the small details of one's daily work, where one has a definite motive for concentration of his attention. If one slights the minor details of his work, he will be sure to slight the more important features. Thoroughness, through concentrated attention, is a virtue of priceless value.

HILL:

But, is it not true, Mr. Carnegie, that busy executives do not spend their time in managing minor details connected with their responsibilities?

CARNEGIE:

Yes, that is true, but you overlook one important fact. The successful executive usually attains his position by having first acquired the art of mastering details. If he remains a successful executive he must continue to be the master of details, but he usually relegates minor details to subordinates who act for him. Thus, by the use of the Master Mind principle, he continues to attend to all necessary details.

A man is paid for that which he does or that which he can influence others to do. The able executive is the man who has so related himself to others that he can increase their efficiency, thereby adding to his own. The man who is clever at getting work done, and done well, by others is worth much more than the man who does it! But, he must know details. If he doesn't, he will not know how to relegate details to subordinates.

HILL:

Does Controlled Attention bring other benefits than those which are available from its application in human relation ships such as you have mentioned?

CARNEGIE:

Yes, many of them! Let us name a few of the major benefits: First, Controlled Attention is the means by which an individual gains control over the faculties of his own mind, through self-discipline. That is important enough to justify all the time one might put into developing the habit of concentration, but there are other advantages.

It is the major means by which all voluntary habits are developed!

It is also the means by which one may eliminate undesirable habits.

It can be used to clear the mind of fear and doubt, thus preparing the way for the exercise of faith.

It is the medium by which the mind may be cleared for prayer, for concentration on a definite desire, in a spirit of faith, is prayer.

All these are benefits an individual may enjoy, through the application of concentrated attention, without contact with anyone.

HILL:

It seems, from your analysis, that Controlled Attention is associated, in one way or another, with every function of both the body and the mind.

CARNEGIE:

That is true! You might well have said it is associated with every function of the mind and the body, and every important human relationship as well. You should observe, also, that Controlled Attention is a degree of self-hypnosis, through which a man can prepare his mind for any reality he has to meet in life. Intense concentration of thought gives one the benefit of the power of that strange state of mind known as hypnotism. Some have used this power effectively in curing certain forms of disease. It can be used to master sorrow and grief and disappointment, where it is applied in conjunction with the power of the will.

HILL:

Isn't Controlled Attention always the result of the use of the faculty of the will?

CARNEGIE:

No, it may be applied through either the faculty of the emotions or the faculty of the will. It may also be applied through a combination of both the emotions and the will. When it is applied by the power of will, it becomes the master of the emotions!

HILL:

And that is the means by which one may place all emotions under the control of the will?

CARNEGIE:

Correct! Intense concentration of the attention upon a given subject, through the aid of the will, leaves the emotions no means of expression. The order can be reversed, as it generally is, and the mind may be so intensely concentrated on a given subject, with the aid of the emotions, that the faculty of the will becomes powerless to operate. The choice between the emotions and the will, in any given instance, is with the individual.

HILL:

Which is the safer choice, the emotions or the will?

CARNEGIE:

The will is safer, provided it is applied in conjunction with the faculty of reason and the conscience. The emotions and reason often disagree. That is one thing that causes trouble for so many people. They allow their emotions to have full sway, without the modifying influence of the reason. The person who has developed a high degree of self-discipline has the power to give expression to either his will or his emotions, or to subdue one in favour of the other, as he chooses. This is the ideal attainment in self-control.

HILL:

From all you have said, I deduce that the sort of thought power which lifts one above the ordinary limitations of fear and sorrow and discouragement is which one attains only by Controlled Attention, backed by definiteness of purpose. Perhaps the leaders who rise above mediocrity and make high places for themselves, in their chosen calling, are those who have acquired the habit of concentrated effort?

CARNEGIE:

Yes, and the best evidence that this is true may be found in the fact that the more successful people of the world, from as far back as we have any records of human achievement, have always been one-idea people. That is, they have acquired an obsession for the attainment of some single purpose, and they have concentrated the major portion of their time and thought upon that subject. It is often a mistake to assume that the term 'one-track mind' is an epithet, for it may connote distinguished honour, instead.

When asked by a friend what he believed to be the greatest human problem, a distinguished philosopher replied, "The greatest problem? Why, the greatest problem by which anyone is confronted is that of learning how to concentrate his thought power on his problems until he burns a hole through them."

With that statement, I fully agree!

It has always been a source of astonishment to me, why so many people waste enough energy worrying about problems when it could enable them to find a solution, if the energy were concentrated upon that definite end.

HILL:

Do people who have a Definite Major Purpose in life, and devote their time to its attainment, worry over problems the same as those without such a purpose?

CARNEGIE: No, they do not! Definiteness of purpose, backed by a plan for its attainment, tends to conserve one's energies for the sole purpose of attaining that purpose. Worry is the brainchild of the man who is not definite! The very moment one decides what action he is going to take in connection with any problem, and begins to carry out his decision, he usually ceases to waste any of his energies worrying over it.

HILL:

Action must accompany decision, however? Decision, without physical action, may still leave one room for worry?

CARNEGIE:

You have the idea correctly. One of the greatest of all forms of concentrated action is that of intense effort, behind a definite purpose, commonly known as work! I have known this to correct physical ailments, and it is the world's finest formula for mental disturbances. Most so-called 'bad dispositions' could be cured through a stiff workout in some sort of physical labour sufficient to work up a good sweat.

Analyse a busy man, in whatever calling you choose, and observe how very little time he wastes over worries. And, if he happens to be a man who has acquired an understanding of the power of concentrated effort, through the coordination of thought and physical action, you will find him spending not one second on worries.

But you will find that he makes decisions definitely and promptly; moves on his own initiative, without supervision or urge from others; has an abundance of enthusiasm; has confidence in himself and faith sufficient to drive him forward in the pursuit of the object of his purpose.

HILL:

Yes, I see now why you say that Controlled Attention is the master key that unlocks the doors to the solution of many problems on the one hand, and unlocks the doors to greater opportunities on the other hand.

CARNEGIE:

That states the matter very clearly! It might also be stated this way: Controlled Attention locks the doors behind things we do not want and opens the door to the things we do want. Therefore, it is a master key in fact as well as in theory.

HILL:

Would it be correct to say that Controlled Attention becomes a master key that locks the doors against things one does not want and opens the doors of opportunity to things one does want, because it conditions the mind for that state of mind known as faith?

CARNEGIE:

That would be literally correct, but Controlled Attention does more than prepare the way for faith; it inspires physical action back of one's faith. It also inspires other success qualities, such as enthusiasm, initiative, self-discipline, definiteness of purpose, creative vision, and organised thought.

Controlled Attention magnetizes the brain with the nature of one's dominating thoughts, aims, and purposes, thus causing one to be always in search of every necessary thing that is related to one's dominating thoughts.

For example, let us say that a man makes up his mind to find a more responsible and better-paying position. From the moment that he reaches a decision in his mind to find such a position, he will find himself searching the 'Help Wanted' columns of the newspapers, and making inquiries among friends. His imagination will become keener and he will begin to devise ways and means of finding what he desires. In proportion as he concentrates his mind on the subject will he extend the scope of his search, until he will eventually find that for which he is searching. It may come from a source he least expects, but careful analysis would be almost certain to prove that it came because of some physical action, or some spoken word on his part.

Concentration on a definite purpose, in a spirit of enthusiasm, puts the subconscious mind to work on establishing ways and means of carrying out that purpose.

I have heard experienced detectives say that rarely is a crime committed that cannot be solved by concentration of attention. Often there is no evidence whatsoever as to who the perpetrator of a crime was, but the seasoned detective can take hold of such a case and, by the simple process of asking questions among those who are familiar with the crime, very soon unearth clues that lead to the solution. Controlled Attention is the detective's greatest aid in the solution of crime. As a matter of fact, many successful detectives have no other outstanding qualification in this field except keen power of observation and the power of intense concentration of their minds. If these two qualities are useful in the solution of crimes – and obviously they are – they are equally helpful in the solution of other sorts of problems.

HILL:

Yes, I can see that alertness in observation might be as helpful in searching for hidden opportunities for self-advancement as it is in the detection of crime. How does one develop the power of alertness of observation?

CARNEGIE:

It is the result of habit based on motive. When a man adopts a Definite Major Purpose and backs it with a strong motive for its attainment, he begins automatically to develop alertness of observation in connection with everything and everyone which may be even remotely associated with the attainment of that purpose. You see, motive magnetises one's mind with a power that attracts everything which affects that motive.

The policeman who walks a definite beat day after day will see much more of what goes on along his beat than will the average person who goes there only occasionally and has no particular reason for observing details in that neighbourhood.

It is said that an Indian warrior or hunter can track a man or an animal through a forest, although no tracks visible to the untrained person are in evidence. He has trained himself, through Controlled Attention, to observe details the untrained person never would recognise, and his motive is that of self-preservation. The Indian becomes alert in the observation of physical details of his environment because his living depends upon it.

Follow the illustration on through and you will observe that most of the so-called 'self-made' men have a keen imagination, initiative, self-reliance and perseverance, and this is due, in the main, to the fact that they were thrown on their own responsibility and forced to develop these qualities. They had a definite motive for the action which led to their success. A man without an obsessional motive is a man without power; or, if by chance he comes into power, he will not be able to hold it.

HILL:

Your illustration seems to suggest that motive may be an important factor in education. The teacher who can inspire the student with the strongest motive for learning might teach him more than the person who endeavoured to force him to study because of fear of failure at examination time.

CARNEGIE:

You have laid your finger on one of the most important factors of pedagogy. And the same theory would apply, in the relationship between employer and employee, or parent and child. The best way to induce anyone to do anything is by the provision of a motive sufficient to attract his attention and arouse his desire.

Take your own mission in life, as an example. Your Definite Major Purpose is to organise and distribute a philosophy of individual achievement. While your job may seem formidable as to its scope and the time required in which to do it, yet you are fortunate in that distribution of the philosophy will appeal to people through practically all of the basic motives. There will be no need, therefore, to try to force its acceptance, because it offers a practical approach to the things all normal people want most, particularly these:

1. Material wealth
2. Love
3. Freedom of body and mind
4. Desire for personal expression leading to fame
5. Self-preservation

Anytime you can offer anyone anything that appeals to him through these five motives you may be sure of its ready and willing acceptance. Here you have five of the strongest motives that move people to action, under the more important circumstances of life. Therefore, no teacher of this philosophy will ever find it necessary to penalise any student of the philosophy in order to influence him or her to study. The motive for study already exists in the minds of all normal adults!

For this same reason no student of the philosophy will find it difficult to concentrate his or her attention on the study of the philosophy. And, you see what an advantage this fact provides the student, because all habits are related to habits of a similar nature. The habit of Controlled Attention in connection with the study and application of this philosophy will develop other habits of concentration that will lead to a series of related motives associated with opulence and personal achievement.

It is this peculiarity as to the multiplicity of motives that will induce people to master and apply this philosophy, and which enabled me to look ahead into the future and foresee that it will gather momentum and become a nationwide influence.

In this fact, you may find your major motive for devoting twenty years or more of temporarily profitless research to the organisation of the philosophy, which you will be compelled to do before it will have been proved and accepted by the public. You, too, will move in response to the five motives I have mentioned, for your work offers reward through each of these.

With this theory in mind, I am now prepared to tell you that the major portion of the remainder of your life will be devoted to the organisation and the distribution of this philosophy. You have already become sufficiently interested in the job ahead of you to enable me to prophesy that you could no more quit your job before it has been finished than a fly could escape from a sheet of fly paper, but not for the same reason. You will stick because you will desire to do so. Your desire is based on at least five strong motives; therefore, you will have no difficulty in concentrating your attention on your job. But you would have plenty of difficulty in trying not to do so.

HILL:

And now, Mr. Carnegie, inasmuch as the philosophy of individual achievement is being organised to serve the people of the United States, will you analyse the opportunities for self-advancement under the American way of life, by explaining why concentrated effort is necessary for individual success under our economic system?

CARNEGIE:

Yes, but the analysis will have to be broken down into many subjects before the real reason for concentrated effort is clear.

We have already explained why an individual must organise his thought power and concentrate it upon one thing at a time, for this is the way to individual self-mastery upon which personal power is based. Let us now turn our attention to the external circumstances with which an individual must deal in his struggle for the attainment of his Definite Major Purpose, or for the attainment of a mere living if his ambition carries him no further.

To begin with, let us observe that the American way of life is founded upon a system of government that was designed to consolidate the power of all the people in such a manner that it automatically provides every citizen with the utmost amount of liberty, personal freedom, and the privilege of marketing his talents, through his own initiative, in proportion to their value as a service to others. Here, then, we begin to see concentration of power on a scale such as does not exist anywhere else; concentration under a system that gives the humblest citizen more rights and privileges and greater opportunities for the accumulation of private wealth than were possessed by kings and potentates of the ages that have passed.

HILL:

The vast variety of opportunities for personal promotion and improvement that exist in the United States is the direct result of the power the people have concentrated in their form of government. Thus, it is the application of concentrated effort, on a huge scale, which provides every individual with the privilege of concentrating upon work of his own choice?

CARNEGIE:

That states the matter perfectly. Concentration of the many provides the privilege of concentration by individuals. Thus, concentrated power becomes a form of insurance against interference with personal rights and property rights, under the greatest system of human relationship known to the world.

Now let us see what the people have done with the privilege they enjoy under this system, for here is where the greatest variety of personal opportunities exist. First, let us recognise that this is essentially an industrial country, the major business of which is the making and the distribution of useful articles. The manufacturing and the distribution are carried on by the people themselves, under an industrial management system known as free enterprise operating under the profit motive. It would not operate for the benefit of all under any other system, for there must be a motive to inspire action in all walks of life.

We have a motive behind our industrial system which is elastic enough to provide everyone connected with it with the necessary inspiration for action based on his best efforts, since the system pays the individual according to his talents, education, experience, native ability, and ingenuity of mind. The system has no stopgaps on individual talent, but it has been so ingeniously designed that it encourages everyone to render the greatest service of which he is capable, knowing, in advance, that his remuneration will be in proportion to the service he renders. This system encourages the development of definiteness of purpose, personal initiative, self-reliance, enthusiasm, imagination, creative vision, organised thought, and the other success principles included in this philosophy.

Now let us see, who owns American industry? We operate under a system of corporations in which the humblest person may own an interest according to his financial resources, and the larger corporations, such as the railroad companies, the steel industry, and the telephone and communication companies, are owned by a cross-section of the people representing almost every type of person in every calling who have invested their savings in the shares of these corporations.

To make it convenient for the owners of the shares to acquire and sell their holdings in these shares, at will, we maintain a stock exchange where anyone may either sell or buy shares in almost any corporation that is listed as having the right to offer its shares to the public. Thus, the ownership of the industries is so flexible that it never remains the same two days in succession.

Here, again, we see concentration on a huge scale: the concentration of the savings of millions of men and women who own the shares of the corporations that operate industry. The shares in the well-managed corporations are so flexible that their owners may use them as collateral for borrowing money at banks in times of emergencies, without losing their interest in the corporation. Thus, one may have his money invested in industry and still have the use of it for other purposes.

The manpower that operates the industries is made up of men known as the 'management' and others known as the 'workers', both of which groups may be also owners in the business, or not, as they choose. Generally, however, a majority of the men who work in both of these groups own shares in the business for which they work. Thus they are, in a broader sense, working for themselves. This is another method of providing men with an appropriate motive for rendering useful service to the extent of their capacity, education and experience.

It is a practice in all the better-managed corporations to leave the door of opportunity for individual promotions wide open to every worker. Thus, no one need remain in a lowly position if he has ambition for a better position, or can develop such ability through his experience.

The system of individual promotion is so efficient that many of the larger corporations have "talent scouts' constantly in search of men who have the ability for leadership. There always has been and perhaps there always will be a shortage of men in the management group, at the top. This condition provides the greatest of motives for the exercise of individual initiative, imagination and alertness on the part of the workers. Never, in the history of mankind, has a more efficient system of human relationship in the field of economics been devised, for it obviously provides every person with an outlet for such talents as he may possess, and it goes much further by providing one with an adequate motive for improving his talents by study and special training courses.

HILL:

It would be correct, then, to say that advancement is rapid and sure for those who master and apply the principles of this philosophy?

CARNEGIE:

To be sure! That is the purpose of organising the philosophy; to enable ambitious people to learn how to concentrate all their energies upon the attainment of whatever station in life they aspire to hold.

Now, sum up all these factors I have mentioned and observe that I have been describing the American way of life, under which every individual may have the use and benefits of his share of the stupendous power of the United States – a power that has been developed by the concentration and harnessing of the people's combined wealth, talents, special abilities, and educational facilities.

HILL:

Can you think of any improvements in the American way of life, and our economic system, which you believe might add to the benefits it provides the individuals who participate in it?

CARNEGIE:

The system is the best that civilisation has yet produced,

and although it is subject to minor refinements, it is basically sound because it provides the utmost of personal liberty, rewards, personal initiative and encourages the utmost of personal ambition by providing every individual with an adequate motive for growth through useful service.

The improvements should be in the method of operating the system, not in the system itself!

HILL:

That is only another way of saying that the improvements should be in individuals and not in the system?

CARNEGIE:

That's the exact idea I had in mind, and the major purpose of this philosophy is to help bring about improvements in individuals, so they may better enjoy the privileges of the American way of life by rendering greater service under the system.

HILL:

You believe, then, that one of the major improvements that an individual could make in himself is that of concentrating all his energies upon some Definite Major Purpose associated with the American way of life?

CARNEGIE:

Yes, that is the purpose of my Philosophy of American Achievement. It is designed to give every individual the fullest possible benefit of the best that has been learned from the experience of the most successful men the American way of life has produced.

The philosophy is a combination of the theory and the practice of sound fundamentals that harmonise with the American way of life. It not only explains what to do in order to achieve individual success, but it also describes how to do it! The entire philosophy is a highly concentrated presentation of the rules of human relationship that are known to be sound and workable because they have been tried and found efficient.

HILL:

What do you believe to be the greatest danger that may disrupt the human relationships under the American way of life?

CARNEGIE:

The greatest danger consists in the philosophy of a small minority of people with socialistic tendencies who wish to break up the power which has been concentrated for the benefit of the people, through the American way of life. These misguided people would have us believe it helpful to decentralise the power that has been accumulated through the consolidation of the money and the talents of the people, under our industrial system.

Instead of our being permitted to pool our savings and use them as operating capital in the management of the corporations, as we now do, the socialists would have us destroy this consolidation of power by dividing it up among individuals, not recognising the fallacy in the fact that no one individual would have enough capital to produce an automobile, or provide a transportation system, such as the railroads, or build a home, or supply any of the other modern luxuries and necessities of life such as we now enjoy under our present standard of living.

Decentralising the wealth of America would be about the same as decentralising the power of the army, by giving every soldier the right to conduct himself independently of the others, thus leading to the destruction of the power that comes from concentrated effort.

HILL:

You believe, then, in concentration of power under a system that functions through chosen leaders?

CARNEGIE:

Yes – chosen leaders; not leaders who have assumed the power of leadership without the consent of those whom they lead. We have, in the American industrial system, the finest example of concentrated power that is administered through leaders chosen by those from whom the power is obtained. This is pure democracy in its finest working order.

The power comes from concentration of the wealth and the personal services of those who operate industry. It is administered by leaders who are chosen by the owners of the operating capital (made up, as they are, of people of all walks of life) known as 'management'.

Here leaders are chosen on the basis of their qualifications for leadership, consisting of their education, experience and native ability. If a mistake is made in choosing any individual leader, it can be corrected from the same source that the mistake is made.

The system under which American industry is operated is similar to the system under which the government operates. The power of the United States (which is the envy of the world) consists of the coordination between our system of government and the other systems of our economic and industrial life, all of which constitute what we call the American way of life.

HILL:

What, in your opinion, Mr. Carnegie, is the greatest tangible virtue of that which you call the American way of life?

CARNEGIE:

Its greatest virtue consists in the fact that it provides all the people with the utmost personal liberty and the privilege of living their own lives in their own way, with the greatest opportunity for self-determination and the accumulation of individual wealth.

Instead of penalising personal ambition and individual desires, as is the case under many other systems that have been tried and are being tried in other countries, the American way of life places a premium on these human traits, by rewarding everyone in proportion to his contributions to society as a whole.

HILL:

One might say, then, that the American way of life is the world's most impressive demonstration of the power of concentration of human endeavour?

CARNEGIE:

That would be stating the facts correctly! Ours is the most powerful government of the world. Ours is the richest country of the world. Our people are the freest people of the world, and the richest as individuals. Our system of economics and our social systems provide the people with more luxury than any other people enjoy, and those of us who adjust our mental attitude to harmonise with the American way of life have more peace of mind than any other people of the world.

HILL:

Your advice to the American people, I assume, would be to let well enough alone, by making the most of the American way of life?

CARNEGIE:

Yes, my advice would be to let the American way of life alone as it is. Those who feel that improvements should be made in any portion of our economic or social system should begin the improvements they recommend by applying them in their own lives. If anyone thinks he can improve the American way of life, let him first demonstrate the soundness of his plan by making it work in his own life. Then the rest of us will be glad to adopt his system, if it proves to be better than our present system.

HILL:

In other words, you would recommend to those who wish to divide up the wealth equally, that they get together, form a colony of their own, and divide up their personal possessions.

Then, after they prove that they can live better and be more prosperous and enjoy more of the luxuries of life than we possess, who believe in and adhere to the American way of life, we may be influenced to scrap our present system and adopt theirs?

CARNEGIE:

That's the idea! But I must call your attention to the fact that many such colonies have been tried already. So far, not one of them has worked, and those who started the idea were forced to come back to our present system, where they could avail themselves of the benefits of the concentration of wealth and personal endeavour, under a democratic system of leadership.

HILL:

What was missing in those collective efforts, which prevented them from succeeding, Mr. Carnegie? It would appear that they were based on concentrated effort, through mutual consent of all concerned.

CARNEGIE:

Many essentials were missing. First, the profit motive, which causes individuals to exert their best efforts and act on their own initiative, was missing. Second, the spirit of self-determination was missing. Take away from a man his desire to become independent and you rob him of much of his initiative, enthusiasm, imagination, and self-discipline. When a man gives up his privilege of independence, he also gives up a proportionate amount of his enthusiasm and ambition. One of the most essential factors that was missing was the power that is acquired through the consolidation of a vast amount of wealth with an equally vast amount of manpower, such as we enjoy under the American way of life.

HILL:

I see what you mean. The socialist experiments have not worked because the individuals engaged in the movement lost the spirit of self-determination that is possessed by the man who moves on his own initiative, fixes his own habits of living, lives his own life, and engages in his choice of occupations.

CARNEGIE:

Well, that was partially the cause of their failure. The important fact I wish to emphasise is this: Socialistic colonies have not succeeded, whereas the American way of life has succeeded! These effects we are familiar with. As to the cause we may disagree, but as to the effects, there can be no disagreement, for the facts speak for themselves.

Even where socialistic colonies have existed for a time, they have not found any method of providing their members with the luxuries of life that the average person enjoys under the American way of life. At most, they have provided the scantiest sort of a living, under conditions which deprive the members of the privilege of personal initiative. Therefore, the members must have been deprived, also, of the peace of mind possessed by the man who lives his own life.

HILL:

Yet there have been many different systems of cooperative societies which seem to have worked pretty well, Mr. Carnegie.

CARNEGIE:

Now you are getting into an entirely different field. Cooperation is vastly different from socialism. The principle of cooperation is one of the principles of the philosophy of individual achievement, under the American way of life; but it has nothing in common with socialism. Cooperation brings benefits without the loss of individual initiative and the right of free enterprise.

Cooperation does not deprive a man of the motive which inspires him to use his imagination, enthusiasm, and creative vision. Cooperation is a part of the great American way of life through which the material resources and the manpower are coordinated so as to produce the greater combined power that is available for the people of America.

There is cooperation in socialistic colonies, but the right motive to produce enduring power is missing.

Controlled Attention, Napoleon, is essential to a democratic free enterprise system, and is discouraged, diminished, and ultimately absent in a Socialist system.

□

How to Own Your Own Mind

Close attention to the chapters of this book will permit the reader to learn what Mr. Carnegie taught me many years ago. One must recognise opportunity through Creative Vision, conceive how to capitalise on opportunity through Organised Thought, and control the mind's activities and direct them to a given end with Controlled Attention. You will then own your own mind and be ready to take necessary action to achieve your goal.

THE HUMAN will can overcome any obstacle, or any handicap, if a man has enough backbone to use it.

THAT SECRET power from within, which has the answer to all problems, can be contacted through concentration of thought based on definiteness of purpose.

WHEN THOMAS Jefferson decided to act, no unexpected obstacle could swerve him from his course; for he had considered carefully and well.

YOU ARE the architect of your own career.

—Frank Channing Haddock

□□□